T0328784

Cambridge Elements ≡

Elements in Philosophy of Law
edited by
George Pavlakos
University of Glasgow
Gerald J. Postema
University of North Carolina at Chapel Hill
Kenneth M. Ehrenberg
University of Surrey

THE PHILOSOPHY
OF LEGAL PROOF

Lewis Ross
London School of Economics and Political Science

CAMBRIDGE
UNIVERSITY PRESS

Shaftesbury Road, Cambridge CB2 8EA, United Kingdom

One Liberty Plaza, 20th Floor, New York, NY 10006, USA

477 Williamstown Road, Port Melbourne, VIC 3207, Australia

314–321, 3rd Floor, Plot 3, Splendor Forum, Jasola District Centre, New Delhi – 110025, India

103 Penang Road, #05–06/07, Visioncrest Commercial, Singapore 238467

Cambridge University Press is part of Cambridge University Press & Assessment, a department of the University of Cambridge.

We share the University's mission to contribute to society through the pursuit of education, learning and research at the highest international levels of excellence.

www.cambridge.org
Information on this title: www.cambridge.org/9781009507394

DOI: 10.1017/9781009127745

First published 2024

A catalogue record for this publication is available from the British Library.

ISBN 978-1-009-50739-4 Hardback
ISBN 978-1-009-12504-8 Paperback
ISSN 2631-5815 (online)
ISSN 2631-5807 (print)

Cambridge University Press & Assessment has no responsibility for the persistence or accuracy of URLs for external or third-party internet websites referred to in this publication and does not guarantee that any content on such websites is, or will remain, accurate or appropriate.

The Philosophy of Legal Proof

Elements in Philosophy of Law

DOI: 10.1017/9781009127745
First published online: April 2024

Lewis Ross
London School of Economics and Political Science
Author for correspondence: Lewis Ross, L.ross2@lse.ac.uk

Abstract: Criminal courts make decisions that can remove the liberty and even the lives of those accused. Civil trials can cause the bankruptcy of companies employing thousands of people, asylum seekers to be deported, or children to be placed into state care. Selecting the right standards when deciding legal cases is of utmost importance in making sure those affected receive a fair deal. This Element is an introduction to the philosophy of legal proof. It is organised around five questions. First, it introduces the standards of proof and considers what justifies them. Second, it discusses whether we should use different standards in different cases. Third, it asks whether trials should end only in binary outcomes – e.g., guilty or not guilty – or use more fine-grained or precise verdicts. Fourth, it considers whether proof is simply about probability, concentrating on the famous 'Proof Paradox'. Finally, it examines who should be trusted with deciding trials, focusing on the jury system.

Keywords: legal proof, evidence law, trials, juries, beyond reasonable doubt

ISBNs: 9781009507394 (HB), 9781009125048 (PB), 9781009127745 (OC)
ISSNs: 2631-5815 (online), 2631-5807 (print)

Contents

Introduction

Criminal courts can remove the liberty and even the lives of those accused of wrongdoing. Civil courts can deport asylum seekers, render companies employing thousands of people bankrupt, and remove children from the care of their parents. Using the right standards when deciding legal cases is therefore of the utmost importance in making sure those affected by trials receive a fair deal.

While legal standards can at first sound like a rather dry or technical subject, the project of deciding on the right standards raises fascinating and deep philosophical questions. These questions cut to the heart of debates about ethics, politics, psychology, and epistemology. Questions about legal standards force us to examine where the state's duty to protect society conflicts with the interests of those accused of wrongdoing. Understanding these debates also reveals how citizens can limit or control legal institutions that wield considerable – and potentially oppressive – power over them. Thinking about legal standards of proof is both a topic of great theoretical interest and one that affects the lives of everyone in society. The standards we use ultimately determine when the state can take away our freedom, our children, our property, and even our lives.

This Element is an introduction to the philosophy of legal proof. It aims to be accessible to students of both law and philosophy, presupposing no technical background in either subject.

The Element is organised around five questions.

- Section 1 introduces the standards of proof and asks what justifies them.
- Section 2 asks whether we should use different standards in different cases.
- Section 3 discusses whether criminal trials should end in binary outcomes – guilty versus not guilty – or whether we should use more fine-grained verdicts.
- Section 4 asks whether proof is simply about showing that something is probable or likely, concentrating on the famous 'Proof Paradox'.
- Section 5 considers who should be trusted with deciding the outcome of trials, focusing on the debate surrounding the jury system.

1 Standards of Proof

Societies use trials to resolve disagreements. These disagreements can be between private individuals, between corporations, and with the state itself. The disagreements can concern any number of issues, from mundane questions about who started a drunken fist fight, to disputes about the arcana of shipping law, questions about the results of an election, or criminal responsibility for murder or rape. Some disagreements end with trivial resolutions like trimming a garden hedge found to be encroaching a neighbour's property. Other disputes end with outcomes of great severity, including the bankruptcy of corporations that employ thousands of people, the overturning of elections, or even the imposition of the death penalty.

Courts must be decisive when resolving disagreements. They must form a view on what happened and deliver a judgement about what should happen next. A court cannot end its work with a 'maybe' and a judge cannot throw up their hands and say they cannot decide one way or the other. Those accused of crimes must be punished or released; election results must stand or be over-turned; at-risk children must be removed from the family home or kept where they are. This burden of deciding is difficult because courts are usually con-fronted with ambiguity. Trial participants often fundamentally disagree – this is why there is a trial! – and point to seemingly contradictory evidence.

Since courts must decide one way or another, they need some method for dealing with evidence and opinions that point in different directions. Courts therefore rely on various rules concerning when something should be taken as 'proven'. While questions about legal proof may sound dry or technical, they are in fact of central importance in legal and political philosophy. Think about it this way: the rules we choose to govern trials are really rules about when the state should use its monopoly of power to force people to do things – to go to prison, to surrender their children, to give up their assets. This section focuses on the most important rules used to decide legal trials – the *standards of proof*.

1.1 The Criminal Standard

A standard of proof is a rule used to determine when the evidence is strong enough for a positive judgement (e.g. finding someone guilty of a crime) to be appropriate. There are different standards of proof. One of the most important distinctions is between the standard used in the criminal law and in the civil law. Criminal proof is the primary focus of this Element, but we will discuss civil proof as we go along. All of this is easiest to appreciate at the level of concrete detail, so let's jump in.

Criminal law ranges over conduct that has been criminalised – such as murder, theft, assault, sexual offences, fraud, and so on. Criminal conduct is usually prosecuted *by* the state (rather than the victim) *against* an individual. Criminal law is distinctive because those judged guilty are open to receive the most serious sanctions available to the legal system. These sanctions are *puni-tive* and can involve the imposition of serious harms on the offender – such as imprisonment or (in some jurisdictions) corporal and capital punishment.

In a criminal trial, the standard of proof used in many jurisdictions is:

Criminal standard of proof = prove guilt *beyond reasonable doubt*[1]

This standard instructs the court to convict the accused of a crime *only if* the evidence supports the guilt of the accused beyond a reasonable doubt. If this standard is not met, the accused must be judged not guilty ('acquitted'). So, the criminal standard specifically governs 'guilty' verdicts, with 'not guilty' verdicts being returned whenever the standard of proof for guilt is not met.

Beyond reasonable doubt ('BRD' for short) is obviously a demanding standard. There are many things supported by good evidence that are nevertheless reasonable to doubt. For example, there may be good reasons to trust your sometimes unreliable friend when they promise to meet you at 7 p.m. for a beer. But it might also be reasonable to harbour doubts. The BRD standard tells us to convict only if there are no reasonable doubts. This means that even if there is some evidence that the accused is guilty – even if you think there is a 'good chance' they are guilty – the court should release the accused so long as there is reasonable doubt. There are much less demanding standards of proof we might use. Indeed, there are other legal standards of proof used outside the trial context. For example, the standard used in different jurisdictions within the United Kingdom to decide whether the police can stop and search somebody is 'reasonable grounds for suspicion'. Clearly, it would be a rather different criminal justice system if criminal courts imprisoned anybody against whom there was reasonable suspicion! Beyond reasonable doubt is a demanding standard of proof.

1.1.1 The *Actus Reus* and *Mens Rea*

Since it will be important later, it is worth saying more about *what* must be proven against the BRD standard to establish criminal guilt. In the 'common law' legal systems we focus on, there are two components jointly required to prove someone has committed a crime.[2] These two components are known by their Latin names – the *actus reus* and the *mens rea*. While the Latin may be unhelpful, the basic idea is pretty straightforward.

First, the *actus reus* is the 'active' part of the crime – the action or conduct that the law prohibits. Here are some rough examples. For theft, the prohibited action is taking the possessions of another without authority, for rape the prohibited action is non-consensual sexual intercourse, for murder the

---

[1] I focus on Anglo-American systems, which have served as the model for many international institutions (like the International Criminal Court). Other jurisdictions use different phrasings for the criminal standard, but generally have a similarly demanding approach.

[2] Common law legal systems are characteristically defined by reliance on what judges have said in previous cases – 'precedent' – to interpret and create law.

prohibited action is causing the death of another person, and so on. Perhaps obviously, criminal conviction requires proving that the accused performed the *actus reus* – the action (or sometimes omission) that constitutes a crime.[3]

Second, the *mens rea* is the 'mental' component of the crime. For example, 'intent' is a common *mens rea* found in the definition of many crimes. For a crime with a *mens rea* of intent, the *actus reus* has to be performed intentionally. This demonstrates where the *actus reus* and the *mens rea* can diverge; for example, someone can cause a death unintentionally. Something is only a crime when there is the right kind of unity between *actus reus* and *mens rea*, between the action that is performed and the mental state underpinning it. There are other mental states beyond intent that can be the *mens rea* for various crimes and we will come back to these later, but this simple account should be enough to go on for now.

To *prove* a crime, the prosecution has the burden of proof to establish *both* the *actus reus* and the *mens rea*, against the standard of proof. So, take the example of theft. To prove the crime of theft you must show that it is beyond reasonable doubt that the accused took the property *and* that it is beyond reasonable doubt that they intended to do so.

1.2 The Civil Standard

Let us now turn to the second main standard of proof, the one used in the civil law.

The civil law regulates the wide variety of non-criminal disputes adjudicated by the legal system. This includes contractual disputes, employment law, corporate law, family law (e.g. disputes about divorce), disputes about 'negligence' (often called torts), and constitutional law. Civil cases can be pursued by almost any person or legal entity against almost any other person or legal entity. In most civil cases, the standard of proof is the following:

Civil standard of proof = prove your case on the *balance of probabilities*

A common way to think about the balance of probabilities is just that it means 'more likely than not'. So, take an example from employment law. An employer should be held liable for breaching their obligations (e.g. failing to provide safety equipment) just so long as the court finds it more likely than not that they failed to provide safety equipment and had an obligation to provide it.

---

[3] A criminal omission might occur where a duty to prevent something is imposed by law – for example, as might apply to public office holders. 'Attempts' can also be a criminal *actus reus*, such as attempting to kill somebody. There are tricky issues in determining when someone has committed a criminal attempt rather than just having a vague plan or intention.

The sanctions that result from losing a civil case are extremely varied. The most common is being compelled to pay compensation. Financial penalties can be vast and serious, leading to bankruptcy or impoverishment. But civil cases cannot generally lead to someone being imprisoned or subjected to other types of punitive treatment. A general rule of thumb in civil law is that compensation aims to provide 'restitution' rather than punishment; it aims to put the party that was harmed in as good a place as they would have been had you not harmed them. For example, the court might try to estimate how much your interests were set back by having your contract breached and ask the other side to make up for it in monetary terms.

Clearly, the criminal standard is harder to satisfy than the civil standard – you can reckon something is 'more likely than not' while still having reasonable doubts. I might think it is more likely than not that my sometimes unreliable friend will turn up for our beer, but due to their track record I may have reasonable doubts. It is entirely consistent for evidence to be strong enough to satisfy the civil standard but not the criminal standard. Indeed, there are instances where this happens. Sometimes people are found not guilty of sexual assault in a criminal court (and hence not subject to punitive treatment like imprisonment) but found liable for sexual assault in a civil court (and hence asked to pay monetary compensation).

1.3 Justifying the Standards

How do we come up with the different standards of proof? In truth, the standards of proof have been heavily influenced by historical circumstance and have evolved piecemeal over time. Especially in common law countries where judicial opinions in individual cases influence the way the law evolves – the system of 'precedent' – the history of legal rules is often convoluted rather than the product of a single design. (Of course, convoluted and complex evolutionary processes do not necessarily make for worse products.) Legal history has, for me, a compulsive nerdish attraction because it shows how fragile and often accidental the way that the law works is. As we will see throughout the Element, it is also a source of stories, where idiosyncratic characters find themselves in the courts and change the way that entire states have operated.

The history of the 'beyond reasonable doubt' standard is much discussed, and the introduction of this terminology happened gradually rather than all at once. The language of 'reasonable doubt' evolved from philosophical discussions throughout the 1600s–1800s that worried about the fact that it might be impossible to prove almost anything with absolute (or 'metaphysical') certainty. (Remember Descartes!) Instead, it was thought that proof of everyday matters, where there is always a chance of error, should be linked to the conscience of the person looking at the evidence; this is sometimes called proving something with 'moral' certainty.[4] From this religiously inflected language, the secular idea of proof beyond reasonable doubt emerged. The connection between proof and the individual conscience will reappear throughout the Element.

As philosophers we are not *primarily* interested in how legal standards came to be the way they are. Rather, we are interested in how they ought to be. We can break this up into two related questions:

(1) Can we reconstruct a justification for the current standards of proof?
(2) In light of how we justify the standards, are they set in the best way?

A natural way to try and justify the different standards of proof is to think about how bad different types of mistakes would be. This is because what standards of proof do, in effect, is strike a balance between different types of error. To see this, consider criminal law.

When criminal courts make decisions – either finding someone guilty or not guilty – they can get it wrong in two different ways. One mistake is *convicting an innocent* person and punishing them for a crime they did not commit. Another type of mistake is *acquitting a guilty* person, allowing a criminal to walk free unpunished. Both of these mistakes are bad, regardless of what type of moral theory you endorse. Convicting the innocent and acquitting the guilty (generally) has bad consequences; the former inflicts misery, while the latter can mean that a dangerous person is released back into the community. It also seems to be unfair even aside from the consequences; the innocent don't *deserve* to be punished, while the guilty might *deserve* punishment. (Of course, this assumes a rather traditional view about the value of punishment. Some might wonder whether punishing the guilty really has good consequences or whether it really is true that those who commit crimes *deserve* to be harmed. While I have some sympathy with this outlook, scepticism about punishment will mostly wait for another day.)

1.4 Two Types of Mistake

Setting the standard of proof involves a balancing act. The harder we make convicting someone of a crime, the less often we will convict people for crimes they didn't commit. Demanding standards provide protection to the accused. However, by making the standard harder to satisfy, we thereby also make it more likely we will acquit people of crimes they *are* guilty of. And, of course, the converse is equally true. The lower the standard, the easier it is to convict; we end up blaming

---

[4] Shapiro 1986.

more people who are genuinely guilty, but also, we make it more likely that we will convict the innocent. How should we perform this balancing act?

One approach might be to suppose that different decisions have some type of expected value or benefit. Then, once we have thought about how large or small these values are, we try to set the standard in a way that would maximise the expected overall value of all the decisions that courts make.

That's quite abstract, so here's an analogy. Suppose you are a fisherman deciding what net to use. You are only after a certain type of fish, red snappers. They are the only fish you can sell at the market; catching other types of fish drains your resources and harms the fish unnecessarily. If you use a very fine net, you'll let fewer red snappers escape, even snappers that are small and difficult to ensnare. But you'll also catch other types of fish too, ones you don't want. If you use a coarser net, you avoid mistakenly landing the unwanted fish you would catch with the fine net, but you also let more precious red snappers get away. What type of net should you use? Well, it depends on the relative value of catching the snappers compared to the expense of catching the unwanted fish. If there's a big difference in value, then we might be justified in using a very coarse or a very fine net. In the criminal law, in effect, we currently use a very coarse net. We leave aside many finer nets – namely, weaker standards of proof – that would catch more guilty people. But why?

1.5 Blackstone's Asymmetry

The following idea by the English jurist, William Blackstone, is often used by way of justification:

Blackstone's asymmetry: It is much worse to mistakenly convict an innocent person than to mistakenly acquit a guilty person.

Blackstone himself suggested it would be *ten times* worse to convict an innocent than acquit the guilty, famously saying: 'All presumptive evidence of felony should be admitted cautiously, *for the law holds that it is better that ten guilty persons escape than that one innocent suffer.*'[5] It's an interesting historical question why Blackstone's 10:1 ratio became the canonical version of the asymmetry known to all law students. In fact, throughout history we find a dizzying number of attempts to formulate a ratio. Even the Book of Genesis contains a passage in which Moses asks how many innocents would have to be present in Sodom in order to

---

[5] Blackstone 1827, book four, chapter 27 (emphasis added).

prevent it from being destroyed by God.[6] But something about the 10:1 ratio has a ring of plausibility. There are ways to build formal models designed to maximise the expected utility of our decisions – a branch of philosophy called 'decision theory' – which suggest that Blackstone's 10:1 ratio recommends a 90 per cent level of confidence as the best level at which to set the threshold for conviction.[7] Intriguingly, 90 per cent confidence in guilt is roughly where some people settle when attempting to quantify the BRD standard of proof. (We'll have more on probabilistic approaches to proof later on.) This 90 per cent confidence level also matches up, roughly, with what some empirical surveys have said about how BRD is interpreted by judges.[8]

However, there is a big question facing Blackstone's seductive asymmetry. How can we justify the claim that it is *much worse* to convict an innocent than mistakenly release the guilty?

One way to think about criminal justice is to focus on what people 'deserve' irrespective of the consequences (a view sometimes called '*retributivism*'). For instance, punishing an elderly criminal whose victims have long since died might be expensive and yield little obvious future-oriented benefit. Yet, some might think that seeking to convict such a person is the just thing to do regardless of whether it leads to any particular beneficial consequences. There are different ways to elaborate on this idea of criminal justice aiming to give people what they deserve. But, it isn't immediately obvious that focusing on what people deserve justifies a very demanding standard of proof. While it is true that convicting the innocent fails to give people what they deserve, so does mistakenly acquitting the guilty. Consider the following. One worry, to which we will return repeatedly as a matter of policy interest, is the low conviction rate for sexual crimes. There is a striking drop-off rate in the number of sexual offences reported to the police against the number that are prosecuted in the courtroom. For example, in England and Wales, a recent report claims that less than 2 per cent of complaints lead to a conviction.[9] One possibility is that the high standard of proof is partly responsible for the low conviction rates for certain types of crimes. Proof beyond a reasonable doubt can be difficult in the context of sexual criminality due to the often private nature of such crimes. If

---

[6] See Volokh 1997 for an entertaining discussion.
[7] On such approaches, see Kaplan 1968; Lillquist 2002.   [8] For example, see Solan 1999.
[9] HM Government 2021, 7. See Thomas 2023 for empirical work on the conviction rate for sexual offences at trial: her findings suggest that criminal trials themselves may not be site of the problem, with conviction rates above 65 per cent in recent years. Of course, the lesson of the low complaint-to-conviction ratio is that many allegations never make it to trial. The standards used in trials influence both police and prosecutorial decisions. For instance, prosecutors will decline to pursue a charge precisely because they believe it is unlikely to meet the standard of criminal proof used at trial.

you think that the 'base rate' of offenders – that is, the number of people who are actually guilty – is higher than the purported 2 per cent being convicted after a complaint, then you might worry that the current standard is preventing these people from 'getting what they deserve'. So, focusing on what people deserve doesn't seem to provide an obvious vindication of using a coarse net.

Another way we might think through this issue is in terms of harm. Does much more misery, pain, and unhappiness result from convicting an innocent person compared to letting a guilty person walk free? It's very hard to answer this in general terms. All crimes are different, all victims are different, and all accused are different. You might be sceptical about our ability to make confident predictions about the amount of harm caused by different criminal justice errors. Still, in many areas of life we can sensibly rely on rough generalisations – it's worse for a doctor to mistakenly amputate your leg than your little finger, and better to cure you of a terminal illness than of a cold. These generalisations can be used to drive policy even if they admit of idiosyncratic exceptions, such as the pianist who would prefer to keep the finger rather than the leg. Perhaps it is *generally* true that more harm results by locking an innocent person up – inflicting a great deal of fruitless misery on them – compared to letting an innocent person go free without them 'getting what they deserve' or being rehabilitated?

A good way to scrutinise a claim like this is to consider an argument against it. Some have worried that we might be setting the standard for conviction *too high* in the criminal law and that we are overlooking or minimising the harms that follow from mistakenly releasing the guilty. Larry Laudan – famous first for his work in the philosophy of science, before turning later in his career to legal philosophy – has used this concern to develop a provocative argument against the BRD standard.[10]

1.6 Consequences-Based Arguments against Beyond Reasonable Doubt

The state has a duty to protect society from harm. When the state releases a guilty person by mistake, it enables a risk of harm to the rest of society. The risk is that the guilty person will reoffend against members of the community. If the court had got it right and found the accused guilty, the person would have been incapacitated through imprisonment. Laudan thinks that the BRD standard skews too heavily in favour of protecting innocent people from the potential harm of false conviction, rather than protecting innocent people from the harms caused by mistakenly released criminals. Indeed, he canvasses criminological

---

[10] The following reconstruction draws on Laudan 2003, 2006, 2011.

evidence – from the US – that purports to show that you are much more likely to fall victim to a violent recidivist than be mistakenly convicted of a crime. From the perspective of someone looking to minimise their own risk, you could use this observation to argue for *lowering* the standard of proof. After all, if the chance of being mistakenly locked up is tiny, but the chance of being harmed by a wrongdoer who could otherwise have been imprisoned is comparatively large, then weakening the standard might seem entirely sensible from the perspective of harm-minimisation.

Laudan's interpretation and use of statistics has been trenchantly criticised.[11] There is also a lot left out by the argument I sketched – for example, assumptions about the underlying ratio of guilty and innocent people, about how frequent different types of mistakes currently are, and about whether mistakes and benefits are distributed unevenly across society. Many of the supposed benefits of identifying the guilty are also controversial and uncertain. Punishment is the main culprit here. Punishment, we are told, has various benefits: it rehabilitates, it deters future wrongdoing by the accused who will wish to avoid repeat punishment, and it deters would-be wrongdoers by making a life of crime generally unattractive. But the empirical evidence on rehabilitation and deterrence, in many cases, does not support these benefits.[12] Often, the threat of harsh sentences seems to do little to reduce crime rates. The same anti-criminal benefit could often be achieved by increasing wages or employment rates. Moreover, prison can even have a criminogenic effect – making people more likely to reoffend rather than rehabilitating them. This is especially true in the many states across the world that have poorly maintained and under-resourced prisons.

Still, even if Laudan's argument rests on shaky or even false empirical claims, the philosophical point remains important. Things can change. If things *were* as Laudan describes them, would this be a compelling reason to lower the standard of criminal proof below 'beyond reasonable doubt'? For example, at one point Laudan suggests a criminal standard of around 65 per cent confidence might be appropriate, a standard not much stronger than the 'more likely than not' standard of civil law.

Laudan's argument is just one of various consequence-based arguments that we could use to criticise the high standard of criminal proof. In addition to the costs imposed by reoffenders, there are various other costs that arguably result from a high standard of proof. Trials cost money and time, as well as being hard on victims, so the legal system tries to encourage those accused to admit their guilt

---

[11] Gardiner 2017.
[12] For meta-analyses on the effects of punishment, see Paternoster 2010; Nagin 2013; Chalfin and McCrary 2017.

before a trial. (Many jurisdictions offer lesser punishments for an early guilty plea and others have systems of 'plea bargaining' where those who agree to plead guilty are charged with less serious offences.) The standard of proof affects the rationality of pleading guilty. The higher the standard of proof, the more rational it becomes for a guilty person to take a gamble and plead not guilty – to try and escape any punishment. Daniel Epps argues that the BRD standard encourages the guilty to 'chance their luck'.[13] If this is right, the overall effect of a high standard of proof is more time and money spent on needless trials, and more guilty people getting lucky and escaping justice. Others discuss the possibility of high standards of proof undermining public confidence in the legal system (because people think too many guilty persons are acquitted) and worry about overly high standards of proof demoralising those responsible for apprehending criminals or encouraging them to use improper methods to gather evidence.[14]

1.7 Defending Beyond Reasonable Doubt?

How can we respond to these arguments? A straightforward way to respond to consequences-based arguments is to fight fire with fire, claiming that the consequences would actually be *worse* if we lowered the standard of criminal proof. Perhaps a lower standard of proof would actually diminish trust in the criminal justice system, because people would perceive it as less accurate? This may be true, but it is hard to be certain that reducing public confidence would have worse consequences than releasing violent reoffenders in the way Laudan complains about. Of course, uncertainty itself may be an argument against making radical changes – if in doubt, it might be best to leave things as they are, given that we have a criminal justice system that functions to some degree. Still, this conservativism is not entirely satisfying.

Another approach might focus on the following fact: one difference between punishing the innocent and the harm caused by reoffending criminals is that the first is actively imposed by the state itself while the latter is just something the state fails to prevent. Perhaps the state is not ultimately *responsible* for harms caused by reoffenders (even though it could conceivably prevent them), while the state *is* responsible for the bad that results from mistakenly punishing the innocent.[15] A large literature exists on the moral difference between 'doing' versus 'allowing'.[16] It is deeply unclear whether this distinction has any general moral significance, so it is therefore not clear whether it can be used to respond

---

[13] Epps 2015. This goes both ways; the lower the standard of proof, the more rational it becomes for an innocent person to plead guilty.

[14] Kitai 2003. Kitai herself isn't ultimately convinced by this worry.

[15] Kitai 2003 defends an argument along these lines.

[16] For example, see Woollard and Howard-Snyder 2022.

to Laudan. Moreover, there are reasons for doubting the usefulness of an actions/omissions-type distinction here. As Laudan himself points out, the state actively *does* something when it creates and sustains a criminal justice system where accused persons are released even when there is reasonably strong evidence they may commit further crimes.[17]

A further point in favour of prioritising protecting the accused is that, in criminal trials, the prosecution has most of the power. The prosecution is backed up by the might of the state, the police, and a skilled cadre of lawyers – in almost all cases, the prosecution has greater resources than the accused. Moreover, as Richard Lippke points out, the defence is at a rhetorical disadvantage. As he puts it: 'Defence attorneys are hired by the accused to represent them, so of course they must say that their clients are innocent. . . . Defence attorneys are apt to be seen as little more than hired guns.'[18] Prosecutors, on the other hand, are in court – in theory – because the state thinks the evidence demonstrates the guilt of the accused. So, the prosecution might benefit from an automatic (and sometimes unearned) trust. An argument for prioritising the interests of the accused is to protect the community from abusive or incompetent exercise of state power. Requiring crime to be proved beyond reasonable doubt is a final protection against such malfeasance. This illustrates a general tension that often arises between two reasonable perspectives within criminal justice and philosophy of law generally. Seemingly compelling arguments that emphasise the importance of the state protecting us from harm (e.g. from criminality), often conflict with another important perspective, namely, the importance of individuals protecting themselves from a state that is too eager to use – and perhaps abuse – its stranglehold on policing and punishment.

This argument against Laudan is promising. But it isn't clear that a very high standard of proof is the best way to protect against the misuse of state power. As I'll discuss in Section 5, the jury system might serve this function irrespective of what standard of proof is used.

It is good philosophical practice to test positions by asking what they would say in more extreme circumstances. So, another way to scrutinise consequences-based arguments for lowering the standard of proof is to consider what they would recommend if the empirical situation worsened. Suppose things were not only as dangerous as Laudan suggests but rather *more* dangerous. Presumably, there would come a point where, according to the logic of Laudan's argument, the underlying empirical situation would not just recommend moderately weakening, but radically weakening, the standard of proof. For instance, recall the 'reasonable suspicion' standard regulating police

---

[17] Laudan 2011, 222.   [18] Lippke 2010, 478.

searches. On Laudan's premises, there may come a point where we would be better off – from the perspective of harm-reduction – endorsing a criminal standard of proof as weak as reasonable suspicion of guilt.

Imprisoning people if there is only a reasonable suspicion of guilt seems unacceptable. Not only does it seem like a recipe for state oppression, it also seems like an objectionable way of sacrificing the interests of an individual accused person for the greater good of the collective. Something in Laudan's perspective, I think, has gone awry.

It is true that we do not use the strongest imaginable safeguards against convicting the innocent. We could use larger juries, always requiring unanimity to convict. We could impose tighter restrictions on when incriminating evidence is admissible (e.g. requiring it be verified by independent sources). We could have automatic post-trial reviews of every conviction. All of these changes would make it harder to convict the innocent. The fact that we don't do these things recognises the fact that we must ensure there is a reasonable prospect of securing convictions. Yet, I think there is a limit in how far we can weaken the safeguards against convicting the innocent before crossing an important moral line.

1.8 Criminal Proof and Community Belief

Rejecting consequences-based arguments for a low standard of proof is different from saying that consequences don't matter for the criminal law at all. We can – and probably should – grant that consequences are generally important in criminal justice. For example, expected consequences might matter for how we should punish people after they are convicted (e.g. punish in a way most effective for rehabilitation) or in setting the rules for granting parole. But, I think that justice requires that we do not appeal to the expected consequences of punishing *until* we have fairly decided whether the person deserves to be punished in the first place.[19] The consequences-based reasons only come into play *after finding the accused guilty* – not when we set the standard of proof used to determine guilt in the first place.

With this thought in mind, I defend a way to think about setting the standard of criminal proof that does not appeal to consequences. We might call the approach a 'blame signalling' view.

Courts play a fundamentally social role – they exist to settle disagreements on behalf of their community. This means that, ideally, the verdicts that courts reach should be an effective social signal that the disagreement has in fact been settled. If the justice system is fair and commands their trust, people in the

---

[19] For a similar thought, see Walen 2015, 427.

community should be able to take the content of a court's verdict as good evidence about the truth of the matter – even if they haven't had the chance to consider the evidence for themselves. (Of course, given the thousands of disagreements that need to be solved by courts, not every citizen *can* consider every case for themselves!) In other words, a court's verdict should ideally be a proxy for what an individual in the community would have believed if they had considered the matter for themselves.[20] To see the importance of this, consider what happens if this *doesn't* happen. If courts regularly found people guilty of crimes but the community did not then believe the convicted were guilty, courts would lose legitimacy. They would not fulfil the role of settling disagreements for the community in question – the guilt of those convicted in court would remain an open question in the mind of the community.

Building on this idea we can make sense of an important idea in philosophy of law. This is the idea that the standard of criminal proof has a close connection with the standards of rational *belief*.[21]

Not all standards of proof have an essential connection to belief. For example, think about the 'reasonable suspicion' standard used for stop and search. Clearly, you can reasonably suspect something is the case without believing it (e.g. you might reasonably suspect your date has stood you up but not quite believe it yet!). But proving that someone is guilty of a crime, I think, ought to be different. You should not find someone guilty without fully believing that they are guilty. But why?

One influential position in moral psychology draws a connection between belief and moral *blame*. For example, Lara Buchak has argued that one thing that is distinctive about belief is the role it plays in legitimating blame. Specifically, Buchak argues that one thing that sets belief apart from other attitudes is that we must believe that someone is responsible for something before blaming them.[22] Let's think about this idea a bit more closely.

In many contexts, we proportion our reaction to the evidence along a spectrum. For example, if it's only 25 per cent likely to rain you act one way (risk shorts and T-shirt), if it's 50 per cent likely to rain you act differently (take an umbrella just in case), and if it's 95 per cent likely to rain you act differently yet again (full waterproofs). Buchak suggests that blame is different – it's an on–off reaction, rather than something we increase or decrease along with the evidence. For example, suppose you know that one of your two children created a huge mess but, until you interrogate them – and see their guilty or indignant faces – you don't know which one it was. Suppose they are both scamps so it's 50 per cent likely

---

[20] I discuss this in Ross 2023a.

[21] I discuss various ways that this idea has been developed in Section 4.

[22] Buchak 2014. Also, see Littlejohn 2020.

either way. The rational thing to do isn't to blame them *both* to a 0.5 degree! Rather, you wait until you have the evidence that allows you to fully believe one was responsible. Buchak concludes that merely having a probabilistic estimate about someone's culpability is not the sort of attitude that justifies blame – *believing that they did it* is the attitude needed for blame.

Criminal courts blame people for breaking the norms of the criminal law. If there's a close connection between blaming and belief in individuals, this might be helpful in our search for a way to understand the standard of criminal proof. Does the belief–blame connection straightforwardly show that the standard of proof needs to be high enough to make sure that the evidence makes it rational to fully believe the accused is guilty?

This is a tempting line of thought, but it's too quick. After all, courts are not the same as individuals. And legal verdicts are not beliefs. Just because an individual might need to fully believe something in order to blame someone, courts are different from human minds. While the standard for blame in an individual mind might be hard (or impossible) to change, we can change the standard of proof at will – a legislator can set the standard of criminal proof at any level they like. So, why would facts about individual blame constrain the courtroom standards of proof?

The answer, I think, returns to the social role of the criminal court. Imagine that criminal courts routinely found people guilty on the basis of evidence too weak to persuade people in the community to believe that the person was guilty. If this was to become common knowledge, there would be a huge tension between the legal system blaming and punishing following a guilty verdict, and the fact that people in society wouldn't personally feel comfortable blaming the accused. This would be a recipe for the criminal justice system to become alienated from the community that it is supposed to represent; courts would no longer be viewed as holding people to account on behalf of the community.

If courts did not aim to bring people to believe in the guilt of the accused – and potentially to blame them – criminal justice would be more like a system of risk management than a moral practice. Sometimes it is acceptable to treat people just as a vector of risk, especially in emergency situations. Suppose there was a highly contagious and fatal disease. In such cases, it might be acceptable to force people into quarantine even if there was only a 50 per cent chance they are infected. But criminal justice, in my view, should not simply be a way of managing risk. A community punishing someone for committing a crime is not analogous to forcing them into quarantine because they *might* have a virus. Rather, criminal justice inescapably involves moral ideas of blame and criticism, where we hold people responsible for falling short in their conduct. If this is right, we need to make sure that the community can get behind the moral judgements made by criminal courts. Otherwise, we would be taking away people's liberty without members of the community being confident enough to judge them blameworthy, even though the very idea of the punishment is predicated on the person *being* blameworthy. Indeed, without belief in the blameworthiness of the accused, it would be hard for a community to view punishment as legitimate. To maintain the apparent connection between moral blame and criminal conviction, we require a standard of criminal proof strong enough to support a community-wide belief in the guilt of the accused. This means that the standard needs to be rather demanding.

That is my argument for a demanding standard of proof, irrespective of Laudan's claims about the harm of reoffenders. Of course, saying that the standard must be strong enough to support belief in the guilt of the accused leaves many questions open. For example, I have not shown that there is any equivalency between 'beyond reasonable doubt' and the standards for rational belief – believing something may not be the same as believing it beyond reasonable doubt.[23] It seems quite plausible that rational belief is necessary for believing beyond reasonable doubt, but not sufficient. We'll get to some of these questions in Section 2. But what we have is a good start, a lower limit on how weak a standard of criminal proof can be before it begins to undermine the very purpose of criminal justice.

1.9 Back to Civil Proof

What about the civil standard of proof? Although I mainly focus on criminal law, proof in civil law is just as socially important and philosophically difficult. One big difference between criminal and civil law is that civil law doesn't necessarily involve the severe punishments of the criminal law. But for most people, their lives and relationships (personal, economic, social) are structured more fundamentally by the wide-ranging rules of civil law than by criminal prohibitions.

The civil standard of proof – 'more likely than not' – strikes a different balance between false positives and false negatives than the criminal standard. Rather than attempting to minimise false positives, the civil standard yields a more even balance of risks. The civil standard of proof could therefore be

---

[23] It is interesting to note that in England and Wales judges are directed to ask jurors to convict only if they 'are sure' of guilt. This state of 'being sure' is regarded, in theory, as the same as beyond reasonable doubt.

taken as indicating *indifference* between false positives and false negatives.[24] Such indifference might indicate, for instance, that the court views it equally important: (i) to avoid mistakenly holding employers liable for negligence as (ii) to avoid mistakenly overlooking employees who are harmed by negligent employers.

There are many cases where indifference between false positives and negatives in civil law seems sensible. For instance, if two suburban neighbours are arguing about whether *A*'s garden hedge is encroaching *B*'s property, we might think that there is no reason to stack the deck in favour of either party. It might be inappropriate for the state to be seen taking sides in a dispute between private parties by – for example – forcing one side to prove their point beyond reasonable doubt.

But in many civil cases, the justifiability of indifference between different mistakes is less clear. Not all cases are between private individuals and often there are inequalities of power that we might want the state to care about. For example, the same standard of proof is used in disputes about garden hedges as in cases involving the removal of vulnerable children from the family home. Perhaps the badness of exposing a child to abuse is roughly equal to the badness of unnecessarily taking a child away from its parents. But this is not obvious.[25] And in other cases, we might think that some mistakes are more harmful than others. For example, in a civil case involving protection of the environment, we might think that failures to identify mass pollution are especially harmful compared to the cost of unnecessarily making a corporation improve its environmental protection practices.

Civil law has a more ambiguous relationship to moral blame than criminal law. Some civil cases do involve holding people responsible for conduct we would ordinarily regard as morally blameworthy. For example, many serious crimes – such as sexual crimes – can also be pursued in civil courts. Moreover, some civil cases, especially in the US, can lead to 'punitive damages' where the losing party does not simply compensate the other side for their estimated loss, but pays an excess as a quasi-punishment. This raises puzzling questions – if we think that blame is the thing that makes the criminal standard so high, why do the same arguments not apply to the civil law? Of course, the fact that current legal practice does not fully fit with our best theories is not always a reason to think the theories are wrong. Legal systems evolve in a piecemeal and sometimes haphazard way; we should not be surprised by the existence of awkward

---

[24] This itself is not clear. Given that *more than one thing* generally needs to be proven to win a civil case, the burden of establishing multiple points on a given standard of proof might make it harder for the party bringing the claim to win.

[25] See *Re. B* [2016] UKSC 4 for discussion in case law.

cases that do not to fit with our general understanding. But the philosophy of civil proof is an area where there is a great deal of important philosophical work still to be done.

2 Proof: Fixed or Flexible?

The standards of proof appear to be surprisingly inflexible. Take criminal law. The very same standard is used to determine guilt for war crimes in the International Criminal Court and for petty theft in your local court. In each case, the standard is proof 'beyond reasonable doubt'. There is a similar inflexibility in many areas of civil law. The same standard is used to decide whether your garden hedge is overgrown and whether the state should remove a child at risk from their family home. In each case, proof is 'on the balance of probabilities'.

From one perspective, such inflexibility might seem fair and reasonable – everyone is treated equally in court, putative genocidal maniacs and petty thieves alike. But from another perspective, it is strange. Generally, when making decisions in our everyday lives, we change our approach depending on the type of decision we are making. You will want to be more certain when making a bet involving a year's salary compared to a £20 flutter on Saturday's football scores, more certain about weatherproofing when buying a house compared to renting an Airbnb.

Just like decisions in everyday life, decisions faced by criminal and civil courts vary in their gravity. It might be hard to specify all the ways in which cases can differ, but it is uncontroversial to say that some cases involve bigger risks than others. For example, a finding of guilt for petty theft might cause the accused to receive a small fine, while for murder it might lead to them receiving a long prison sentence or even the death penalty. This raises the question: should the legal system use different standards for different cases? We will focus on criminal law primarily. So, we begin by asking: should criminal justice systems use different standards for different crimes?

2.1 Different Standards for Different Crimes?

The idea that some crimes require special treatment has a long history. Consider the crime of treason, which historically came with liability to especially gruesome punishments – most infamously, being hung, drawn, and quartered. For long periods in the history of English law, you could only be convicted of treason through the testimony of *two* eyewitnesses, a rule not applied to other crimes. Curiously, this remains codified in the US Constitution – the drafting of which was influenced by English legal tradition – where it still requires the testimony of two witnesses to convict someone of treason.[26]

The eighteenth century Italian jurist Cesare Beccaria supposed that serious crimes were less common, and so we should require more evidence to be convinced that someone has committed one.[27] For example, it is presumably less common to be a serial killer than a petty thief. (But there do seem to be clear exceptions to Beccaria's claim. Sexual assaults are regarded as very serious, yet many think they are not especially uncommon.)[28]

Beccaria's larger point seems not to be that we should use a higher standard for some crimes compared to others. Rather, he suggested that the empirical distribution of criminal tendencies makes it rational have more default scepticism about the suggestion that someone has done something especially terrible. (Compare: it might be *harder* for me to be convinced that my laziest student managed to ace the exam, but this doesn't mean I should use a more demanding standard when grading their work compared to other students.) This means that everything Beccaria says is compatible with the current 'beyond reasonable doubt' standard. His point is just that doubts are more reasonable when someone has been accused of something especially nasty.

But this raises an interesting psychological question – do people tend to *interpret* 'beyond reasonable doubt' differently in different contexts? This isn't something that judges or juries are explicitly instructed to do. But it is not implausible that people will change what they count as a reasonable doubt depending on the type of crime they are considering. This raises the question, if judges or juries *do* interpret the standard differently across contexts, what factors are their interpretations sensitive to? Is it (just) the statistical rarity of different crimes? The severity of the punishment? The extent to which the victim was harmed? One's emotional reaction to the case? Something else? Some of these possibilities would seem to involve raising the standard for certain crimes, going rather further than Beccaria's suggestion to pay attention to the relative rarity of the crime being alleged.

As philosophers, we are not best equipped to answer questions of psychology.[29] But we can consider whether we should endorse or reject certain psychological tendencies that people have when approaching the standards of proof. To do this, we must ask the larger moral and political question – should we design the legal system so that it has multiple standards of proof, using different standards for different crimes? For example, some suggest that capital (death penalty) crimes should be accompanied with a higher standard of proof

---

[26] US Constitution, Article III, Section 3, Clause 1.   [27] Beccaria 1995.

[28] This point is made by Pundik 2022, who provides a helpful discussion of Beccaria's argument.

[29] Although this often does not stop us trying.

than other crimes.[30] If this is right, that we should use different standards for different crimes, what factors should justify the use of stricter or less strict standards?

A first consideration is whether there is some value in the equality of all crimes being judged against the same standard. I have heard it suggested that the right to a fair trial or treating everyone 'as equals under the law' might require using the same standard for all crimes. But giving everyone a fair trial or treating them as equals doesn't require *identical* treatment. People can share a right to a fair trial, yet this right can be realised in different ways. For example, in some jurisdictions, only comparatively serious crimes receive trial by jury, with less serious offences being decided by a single judge. It is generally true of rights that they can be realised in different ways, depending on the risks and contextual facts of the situation. A right to health, for example, might be shared among all citizens – yet, it is still appropriate to use different standards and procedures when dealing with some patients (e.g. because their disease is especially serious or contagious) than others.

A different argument for using the same standard across all cases concerns public perception. It might undermine public confidence in certain trials if it were widely known that it is easier to get convicted of (say) sexual assault compared to murder or fraud – these might come to be viewed as second-class convictions, unreliable in the eyes of the public. This is an important worry. But it is also true that public confidence is compatible with some variation in the procedures used to judge guilt. Again, some jurisdictions have both trials with juries and trials with judges. This split system – variations of which are found across the world – does not seem to fatally degrade confidence in the criminal justice system. Nor does it seem to degrade public confidence that civil law has a lower standard of proof than criminal law; people are often happy to talk as if civil cases have been 'proven' in much the same way as they do in criminal cases. So, while public confidence is a relevant concern, it isn't the end of the conversation either.

Let's revisit the traditional idea from Blackstone that helped us to analyse the beyond reasonable doubt standard (Section 1.5): 'All presumptive evidence of felony should be admitted cautiously, *for the law holds that it is better that ten guilty persons escape than that one innocent suffer.*' People often use this statement to justify a single 'fixed' BRD standard. But this famous quote is much more plausible when interpreted as *relative* to different types of crime. For example, it may be plausible to prefer letting ten guilty murderers go free than mistakenly putting one person to death after being falsely convicted of

---

[30] See Sand and Rose 2003.

murder. But it is much less plausible to think it better to let ten guilty murderers go free than to mistakenly give somebody a £100 fine for being falsely convicted of stealing a chocolate bar. We can press the worry further. Suppose there *is* some rough number of murderers that we should prefer to go free rather than wrongly convicting one person of murder. Why should we think that this same number applies to other crimes – that the same balance appropriate for murder also applies to theft, sexual crimes, fraud, arson, and so on?

Indeed, if we return to the consequences-based arguments discussed in the previous section, the justification of a single standard becomes even less obvious. The prospective costs of different types of error – releasing the guilty and convicting the innocent – will vary across different types of case. For instance, Larry Laudan's argument for lowering the standard of proof focuses on predicted recidivism rate. This is precisely the type of thing that changes with the type of crime. For example, statistics from England and Wales suggest that 30 per cent of those convicted of knife-related crimes are reoffenders who have committed similar offences in the past.[31] By contrast, those convicted of rape tend to have comparatively low reoffending rates.[32] Although Laudan pitched his argument as lowering the standard of criminal proof across the board, it actually better supports the idea that it should be *lowered for certain crimes*. After all, his point about high recidivism rates and risk of harm only drew on considerations about violent crimes – not (say) economic crimes. Laudan's argument, if you accept his premises, really just gets you to the conclusion that we should lower the standard of proof for some crimes.

This point generalises to other arguments that try to set the standard of proof by looking at the consequences of error.[33] For example, consider the things that vary between crimes:

- Some crimes are met with higher punishments, so punishing the innocent is comparatively worse.
- Some offenders are more likely to reoffend than others.
- Some types of reoffending are more harmful to the community than others.
- Some offenders are easier to rehabilitate.
- Some crimes are more susceptible to deterrence.

---

[31] See GOV.UK website, 'Knife and Offensive Weapon Sentencing Statistics: July to September 2022' (Main Points, 3rd point). https://bit.ly/3TpRFI2.

[32] For example, Freedom of Information data suggests that 4 per cent of rape convictions between 2013–2017 were against those with previous convictions. See Full Fact 2019.

[33] For consequences-based arguments for having different standards for different crimes, see Lillquist 2002 and Ribeiro 2019.

- Some crimes have unusually low conviction rates.
- Some crimes are higher-profile and convictions send out a stronger public message.

If we take a consequences-based approach, given the many ways crimes can vary it seems unlikely that requiring the same fixed level of confidence before convicting would optimise the risks in every single case. The consequences-based approach instead supports a much more flexible approach to proof, where the standard used for a given crime type is sensitive to the listed factors. If we accept this way of thinking, then we should use different standards for different crimes, depending on the expected consequences associated with each.

Is this a plausible approach? Earlier, we tested the merits of consequences-based thinking by taking the view to its logical conclusions. We can do the same for the consequences-based perspective on using different standards of proof for different crimes.

Suppose that some very serious crime type like murder or rape happened to be high-profile, have very high reoffending rates, be amenable to rehabilitation and deterrence through long punishment, and be particularly upsetting to the community. In this case, the benefits of convicting the guilty are raised compared to the costs of punishing the innocent. On the line of thinking we are considering, this would mean that the standard of proof for these serious crimes should become *lower* relative to other crimes. (Convicting more people would allow us to pluck the low-hanging fruit of the benefits I just stipulated.) However, it seems perverse to have a legal system where what we traditionally regard as the most serious crimes that come with the harshest punishments are assessed against *weaker* standards than more trivial crimes such as petty theft.[34] Something seems to have gone wrong with this way of thinking, if the consequences-based approach could license using a lower standard for murder or rape than for petty theft. We need a different perspective.

2.2 Another Perspective on Flexible Proof

In Section 1, I outlined a view on which the criminal standard of proof should support rational belief in the guilt of the accused. Can we use this belief-based theory to make progress on the debate about using multiple standards of proof? To answer this question, we need to consider the relationship between rationally believing something and strength of evidence.

---

[34] I have made this argument in Ross 2023b, where I develop my view on multiple standards of proof in more depth, arguing that we should use more demanding standards for crimes with the severest punishments.

There is some threshold of evidence required for it to be rational to believe something (given the evidence: don't believe in Flat Earthism; do believe in anthropogenic climate change). But does this threshold change depending on the situation? Epistemologists – those who study belief and the evaluative concepts used to assess beliefs – are engaged in long-running debate about this question. A key fault line in their debates is whether the rationality of believing something depends on the practical consequences of being right or wrong.[35]

One view is that practical consequences make *no* difference to what it takes for a belief to be rational; only 'intellectual' considerations determine whether you should believe something. Some call this view *intellectualism* about belief. The opposite view is that the rationality of believing something *is* affected by the practical consequences associated with the belief (and what happens if you have the wrong belief). Take a mycological example. Will a sensible person require *stronger evidence* to rationally believe that a red-and-white dotted mushroom is safe when they plan to eat it, compared to just believing it is safe while walking past it on a countryside ramble? Cases like this motivate some to argue that the practical consequences (or 'stakes') influence the strength of evidence needed to rationally believe something – the greater the harm if your belief is wrong (e.g. eating the mushroom and dying), the more evidence it takes to rationally believe (e.g. the mushroom is safe). Some call such views *stake-sensitive* theories of belief.

If intellectualist views about belief are right, then the belief-based theory of criminal proof isn't particularly supportive of using different standards for different crimes – since none of the practical consequences matter when forming a belief, the different benefits and risks of legal error don't impinge on the standards required to believe the person is guilty. But *if* stake-sensitive views are correct, then a belief-based approach to criminal proof ought to be sensitive to some of the practical differences between convictions and acquittals for different types of crime. In my view, stake-sensitive views are attractive because they consider the close relationship between believing something and being in a position to act on it.[36] A canonical role that belief plays is to guide our behaviour, so it's natural to think that the standards for believing rationally should be influenced by the results of the action that the belief will license.

When it comes to convicting people of crimes, the practical 'stakes' can be divided into two categories, corresponding to different mistakes we can make. The first is the risk to the accused of convicting them when they are actually

---

[35] See Kim 2017 for a summary. My contribution to this debate is outlined in Ross 2022.

[36] There are also difficult challenges for stake-sensitive views. For example, see Worsnip 2021.

innocent. The second is the risk to the community if we release someone who is actually guilty.

Given the second type of risk, it might seem that thinking about the stake-sensitive nature of belief just recreates Laudan's argument: that it is rational to believe something (that someone is guilty of a violent crime) on the basis of weaker evidence, if the consequences of error (mistakenly acquitting a criminal) are particularly bad (they are likely to reoffend and harm society). If this is the right way to understand how the stake-sensitive theory applies to criminal proof, then we haven't made much progress; we have just recreated the implausible conclusion that we could find someone guilty of (say) murder based on weaker evidence than convicting them of petty theft.

Fortunately, this is not the best interpretation of what the stake-sensitive view means for criminal proof. I agree that some risks should make us require stronger evidence before judging someone guilty. In particular, if someone is due to be punished particularly harshly, I think this should make us want stronger evidence. The harsher the punishment, the more confident we should be before we convict someone, given the increased risk of harming them if they are innocent.[37] But my view is that the risks of false negatives (mistakenly releasing the guilty) are *not* a reason to lower our standards. So, the fact that someone might be at an increased risk of reoffending does not make it rational to blame them on the basis of weaker evidence than you would normally require. This is a bit abstract, so it might help to have an example. The view I defend generates the following pattern:

Accept: Greater confidence before convicting someone of x because the punishment for x is death.

Reject: Lower confidence when convicting someone of y if y-guilty people have a high average recidivism rate.

One way to test whether this idea is plausible is to consider the following thought experiment. Compare a really harsh legal system with a more lenient system. Suppose country A cuts off a hand for theft while country B only imposes a fine. Should judges in country A require stronger proof before convicting thieves than judges in country B? My judgement is that the answer is yes.[38] But why?

---

[37] For more detail, see the argument developed in Ross 2023b.

[38] Some 'natural experiments' might support this view. When transportation and the death penalty were removed as sentences in England, the conviction rate increased (see Bindler and Hjalmarsson 2018). However, this evidence is ambiguous. Another explanation, to which we will return in Section 5, is that these were cases of jury nullification of unjust punishment rather than the jury not being convinced that the evidence was strong enough.

The underlying rationale for this judgement is that the risk of false negatives is not directly relevant to the belief-eliciting role of criminal courts. When a court convicts someone, they are sending out a signal that it is acceptable to blame and punish the person in question. This means that the court must be interested in the possibility that they are inducing a community to blame and punish someone undeservedly. The more severe the blame and punishment, the more cautious the court should be – hence a higher standard of proof should be used. However, when a court finds someone *not* guilty, the court isn't in fact saying anything about whether people should believe the person will not commit crimes in the future.[39] Rather, the court is *only* saying that the evidence isn't strong enough to blame and punish the person for the particular thing they are being accused of. So, the risk of false negatives is in this sense irrelevant to the social signalling role performed by a criminal court. In Section 3 I will problematise this view by exploring the idea that courts should proactively 'clear the name' of the accused and support the belief that they are definitively innocent – rather than taking the more restricted role of just saying the evidence isn't strong enough to blame the accused in the current case. This is a question for the next section. Nevertheless, given the *current* social role of the court, we can deny that the risk of releasing the possibly guilty is relevant to the beliefs that courts are tasked with supporting among the community.

2.3 Radically Flexible Standards?

Our discussion has focused on what is at stake in trials about different *types* of crime. However, there is an even deeper challenge we have not yet discussed.

Not only do different *types* of crime differ in the prospective costs of different errors, but so do *instances* of the same crime type. For example, two people accused of murder might have different risk profiles for the future, they might face different degrees of punishment (e.g. because one is a repeat offender), one might be more amenable to rehabilitation, or be more likely be harmed by a lengthy punishment (suppose they have young children). Not only do the characteristics of suspects change, but so do the characteristics of the crimes they are accused of. One murder can be much more violent or high-profile than another; one might come with a particularly harsh sentence or be particularly egregious in the community in which it occurs. Since every criminal accusation has its own unique profile, this poses an even deeper challenge to the idea that the law should use a one-size-fits-all approach to setting the standard of proof.

---

[39] For example, the court isn't saying that it would be inappropriate to take precautionary steps in future dealings with the person (see Ross 2021a for more discussion).

Initially, it is tempting to dismiss this challenge by saying that – although philosophically interesting – the practical obstacles to *explicitly* formulating different standards for each trial render this issue merely academic. Convenience, economy, and the limitations of human effort must place a cap on how tailored criminal justice can be. However, the rise of artificial intelligence and algorithms challenge even this thought. A huge literature has arisen on the pros and cons of using algorithmic tools in criminal justice. They promise to eliminate the idiosyncratic biases of human reasoners,[40] but at the same time have been claimed to risk entrenching demographic biases in sentencing and parole decisions.[41] One thing such tools might allow is for decision-making to be customised in ways that is currently impossible. A question for the future is whether this is a road we wish to travel.

To come full circle, let's return to our earlier comments on *interpreting* the standards of proof. It might be that juries and judges interpret 'beyond reasonable doubt' differently, depending on the context. Given this possibility, perhaps accounting for variation between cases might not require *explicitly* formulating different standards of proof. Since the law uses rather general phrases like 'beyond reasonable doubt' when instructing judges or juries, there is some latitude for the judge or jury to approach the case at they see fit; they are deciding the case against a vague standard, not an extremely precise test. It might be that the current approach is *already* a very flexible one – where cases are judged under the broad banner of 'beyond reasonable doubt' but where the meaning of this is interpreted differently depending on the case and the judgement of the judge or jury about what contextual features matter.

This illustrates two very different ways to think about setting the standards of proof. One is a 'top-down' approach, where the legal system evolves or is designed so that individual judges and jurors are explicitly instructed in what the right standard to use is – where the aim is for cases to be judged as uniformly as possible. Another approach rejects the top-down method of deciding in advance what standard should be used in a given case, but rather leaves the decision about the appropriate standard *in the hands of those who are adjudicating the case*.[42] In this latter sense, there is no prior fully determinate decision about the standard of proof, but rather the standards of proof emerge from a patchwork of individual decisions made by fact-finders on the ground hearing cases every day.[43] From this patchwork of individual decisions made by those who

---

[40] For example, see Sunstein 2021.

[41] One example is the extremely high-profile critical report found in Angwin et al. 2023.

[42] For further discussion, see Loeb and Molina 2022.

[43] 'Fact-finder' is the legal term for the person who decides whether the standard of proof is met – the judge or the jury depending on the type of case.

decide particular trials, the standards of proof emerge. This 'bottom-up' way of thinking about proof entrusts a great deal of responsibility to those who decide cases, relying on their judgement about what the appropriate way to think about the case is. To return to the phrase with which we began this section, it would mean that each judge or jury has to make up its own mind about what is required for an accusation to be proved to a 'moral' certainty.

3 Should Proof Be Binary?

Legal proof is usually conceived as a binary. Consider the words of Lord Hoffmann, an influential English judge:

> 'If a legal rule requires a fact to be proved ... a judge or jury must decide whether or not it happened. There is no room for a finding that it might have happened. The law operates a binary system in which the only values are 0 and 1. The fact either happened or it did not.'[44]

The first paragraphs of this Element were highly sympathetic to Hoffman's description. I suggested that courts cannot shrug their institutional shoulders and that 'maybe' was no use in legal adjudication. In criminal cases, which we continue to focus on, trials end with somebody being convicted or acquitted. Although we've discussed how criminal proof might be flexible by using stronger or weaker standards in different situations before convicting somebody, we haven't yet questioned the *binary nature* of legal decisions. However, there are deep questions about whether this binary system is the best way to approach legal proof.

3.1 Binary versus Non-Binary Systems

Binary legal systems predominate across the world. These are systems in which criminal trials end in either a single 'Guilty' verdict or a single verdict of acquittal (usually phrased as 'Not Guilty').

But not all jurisdictions use a binary system of proof. In Scotland, for example, a 'third verdict' called *not proven* has existed for several hundred years.[45] *Not proven* exists alongside *guilty* and *not guilty* as a separate option for the court. Not proven is the verdict returned when the judge or jury is not satisfied with returning a not guilty verdict, but also cannot find the accused guilty beyond a reasonable doubt. In this sense, not proven is what we can call an *intermediate verdict*. The not proven verdict officially leads to the same outcome as not guilty – the accused is released without punishment. However,

---

[44] *Re B* [2009] 1 AC, para. 2.
[45] There are plans to abolish this verdict, and at the time of writing it seems likely that it will be abolished.

this does not mean that the *informal* consequences are the same – and, as we will explain, the verdict may not have the same social meaning. There is also an intermediate verdict in Israeli law, which has two types of acquittal; one is a 'regular' acquittal, while a second is an 'acquittal on the basis of doubt', where the doubt refers to doubt about the guilt of the accused. In both cases the accused is released, but doubtful acquittals can lead to diminished rights to compensation for false imprisonment, among other consequences.[46]

Legal history also describes non-binary systems of proof that have been abolished. Some of these are not as benign for the accused as the Israeli or Scottish systems. Federico Picinali describes systems with intermediate *punishments* to go along with intermediate verdicts, such as in the *ius commune* that predominated across Europe for centuries following the rediscovery of Roman law in the form of Justinian's Digest in the early 1000s.[47] This system permitted 'extraordinary punishments' that were less severe than the ordinary punishment for the crime. But they served up a stiff penalty for an intermediate confidence in guilt, as the penalties could include exile. Examples from the distant past aside, Italy retained a third verdict until near the end of the twentieth century, a verdict that allowed an official 'criminal record' to be kept regarding the acquitted person and could justify additional measures such as surveillance.

One could mistakenly suppose that intermediate verdicts are a mere curiosity. In fact, thinking about the strengths and weaknesses of different intermediate systems cuts to the heart of fundamental questions about the proper role of criminal justice. Despite these intermediate verdicts raising fascinating questions about legal philosophy, they are a surprisingly understudied phenomenon – both theoretically and empirically. As we will see, it is far from obvious that a binary system really is best.

3.2 Motivating Non-Binary Systems

To see the appeal of non-binary systems, we must think more carefully about what binary systems involve. There's a common misconception that courts either find people guilty or *innocent* of what they are accused of. But this is wrong. Technically, courts only find people *not guilty* when they decline to convict them. Now, this might sound exceptionally pedantic. But these ways of thinking about the court's role are crucially different.

Putting the point in abstract terms, saying that a standard for judging that x is not satisfied is very different from saying that the evidence supports not-x.

---

[46] For discussion, see Vaki and Rabin 2021.

[47] See Picinali 2022 for insightful discussion of all the systems mentioned in this paragraph.

Consider an example. Suppose I plan to climb a mountain at the weekend. The mountain is dangerous, so I adopt the following standard: I will only climb if I think it is >90 per cent likely to stay dry. Now, if the weather forecast shows that this standard is not satisfied, this doesn't mean that it is 90 per cent likely to rain! Rather, it just means that it is at least 10.1 per cent likely to rain. The same is true about verdicts in criminal courts. Just because we don't find someone guilty after judging evidence against a very demanding standard of proof (e.g. 'convict only if you think their guilt has been proven beyond reasonable doubt'), this doesn't mean the evidence suggests that they are – or are likely to be – innocent. Finding an accused person not guilty is compatible with *a broad range of confidence in their guilt*; it only rules out the very highest levels of confidence in guilt. You can think that it is rather likely that someone is guilty while properly acquitting them.

Is it a problem that there is so much variation in how an audience can interpret a not guilty verdict? To answer this question, we might try to see things from the perspectives of two different parties affected by criminal justice.

> *'The perspective of the accused'*. Suppose you are accused of a serious crime. You maintain your innocence. There is a trial – you are found not guilty. But being found not guilty is different from being found innocent, so you feel you have not managed to 'clear your name'. Employers and acquaintances view you with suspicion, thinking there can be no smoke without fire. All you can truthfully say is that the verdict demonstrates the court did not think your guilt had been proven beyond a reasonable doubt. Being found not guilty in a criminal court doesn't prevent people from treating you in ways that reflect their suspicion of you. For example, you might still lose your job in a school even if found not guilty of sexual misconduct, or you might not be hired for a banking job even if even if accused but not convicted of fraud.

> *'The perspective of the community'*. Someone in our community has been accused of a serious crime and found not guilty. However, we don't know how to react to this finding. On the one hand, perhaps the person was simply the victim of mistaken identity and poses no risk to us. On the other hand, perhaps the person only narrowly escaped being convicted, because the evidence against them was strong but not quite strong enough to convince everyone on the jury. We are caught between the temptation to protect ourselves and a concern not to punish them for a crime they have not been convicted of. We waver between the two interpretations, neither fully reintegrating nor rejecting the accused.

Perhaps you care more about one of these perspectives. However, the two complaints are really the same – binary-verdict systems do not provide enough information. Trying to solve the problem of one perspective will also address the complaints of the other perspective.

A non-binary system of proof would address these complaints by removing ambiguity in what an acquittal means. By giving the court additional options, we learn something extra about what the judge or jury made of the evidence. Consider the 'not proven' verdict again. It's a verdict that lies between guilty and not guilty. If the court returns a not proven verdict – interpreted as an intermediate between guilty and not guilty – we learn that they are *not* willing to say that the evidence strongly supports the guilt *or* the innocence of the accused.[48] The existence of additional verdicts also enriches the information provided by the 'regular' verdicts. For instance, if a court returns a 'not guilty' verdict in a system where they could instead have returned a not proven verdict, we also learn something; namely, the court has *declined* to use the not proven verdict and must be happy to say that the evidence supports a not guilty verdict. To summarise, systems with more than two verdicts have an *informational richness* lacked by binary systems. This means that someone found not guilty in a system with multiple verdicts might feel that they have better cleared their name – and the wider community can also feel more reassured about the weakness of the evidence supporting guilt.

Of course, once a legal system decides to abandon binary verdicts, this raises difficult questions about the rules that should be used for choosing a verdict. Having more than two verdicts means that it's possible that no specific verdict is a majority or even plurality winner among the jury, even if there is an odd number of jurors. Indeed, there can even be 'preference cycles' where no single verdict wins a Condorcet-style competition.[49] But these are not insuperable difficulties – the fact that there are existing and successful non-binary systems demonstrates that they do not create huge practical problems.

Intermediate verdicts are just one way to make criminal courts more expressive. There are other ways to speak to some of the same concerns, adding more information to trial decisions. Currently, criminal verdicts are not accompanied by any written justification. But throughout history, courts have not just provided verdicts of guilty and not guilty, but also given reasons or explanations for their decisions. This system of 'reasoned verdicts' gives the judge or jury the chance to express how confident they are in the innocence of the accused when they deliver an acquittal in the context of a regular binary-verdict system. This is an extremely interesting approach with its own particular strengths and

---

[48] An oddity of the Scottish system is that judges offer no guidance on when to return a not proven verdict. Therefore, my comments are a reconstruction of what the verdict should mean.

[49] Bray 2005 discusses preference cycles, alongside a helpful general discussion of the advantages of intermediate verdicts.

weaknesses – I invite the reader to further consider these.[50] For now though, I continue to focus on non-binary systems of proof.

We have been considering the idea that the information-poor nature of binary systems leaves those acquitted open to social stigma and other adverse reactions. But perhaps we should see courts as having a more limited role, one that does not purport to care about social stigma? On a restricted conception of their role, courts *only* inquire into whether the evidence against the accused is strong enough to blame and punish them, taking no interest in social reactions to criminal proceedings beyond this. Indeed, one might have concerns about the idea that legitimising stigma – as might happen when an intermediate verdict is returned – is any business of the court. Court-sanctioned stigma, after all, is different from stigma that exists simply because private individuals put their own interpretation on a verdict. Perhaps by getting into the business of actively licensing social stigma, we invoke the extra worry that courts could actively harm the innocent in cases where an intermediate verdict licenses the stigma of someone who is truly innocent. Moreover, perhaps the state does not wish to facilitate employers or potential relationship partners from rejecting accused persons on the basis of accusations that haven't been proven on the high standard of criminal proof. (Although, when it comes to intimate relationships and susceptibility of partners to harm, one might well one might well think that excluding people who are quite likely to be guilty is perfectly reasonable.) These are valid concerns and much depends on how you view the proper role of the court. But we must bear in mind that harming the innocent via stigmatisation *already* occurs when we acquit an innocent person who is stigmatised due to the informational paucity of a binary system. This is something that most criminal justice systems enable, even though there are alternative systems available with multiple verdicts.

3.3 Worries about Non-Binary Systems

Let's consider whether we lose anything by trying to enrich the legal system with non-binary verdicts.

One important value we keep returning to is public confidence in criminal justice. We want citizens to trust courts. Might having more than two verdicts – going beyond the binary – make people trust the criminal justice system less? Perhaps having intermediate verdicts could be seen as publicly admitting that courts are not always fully confident in their decision to let someone go or to punish them, making transparent the fallibility of trials.

---

[50] For discussion and defence of reasoned verdicts, see Coen and Doak 2017.

This is not, in my view, a decisive worry. Any sense of infallibility that courts enjoy is illusory – we should not cultivate the idea that the public resemble uneducated peasants trembling before the infallibility of a Leviathan. Public confidence in criminal justice should not be secured by *misunderstanding* the nature of the law and what it can reasonably achieve.

Another related reason to be suspicious of non-binary approaches is that they sound like a 'cop-out' – a failure to decide rather than decisively settling the case one way or the other. While this reaction is tempting, I am not convinced it is right. It may be easy to hear an intermediate level of confidence as indecision or an invitation to continue investigating the subject – that is, saying you haven't made your mind up *yet*. But this isn't a necessary part of what it means to adopt an intermediate level of confidence in something. Taking an intermediate or uncertain attitude about a question can be a fully rational and indeed definitive response to the available evidence. Suppose someone wants to make a bet over a coin flip (the coin is regular; a fair coin). Before flipping, I ask whether you believe you will win. The only rational answer is to say you are not sure – that your level of confidence is in the middle or that you are suspending judgement. Given the available evidence, and indeed *given all the evidence there could be* (unless you develop supernatural powers of foresight), this is the right thing to say. In fact, it is the only sensible thing to say. Moreover, having an intermediate level of confidence is not necessarily a prelude to further inquiry. If all the evidence has been gathered and it doesn't decisively point one way or the other, then remaining in an intermediate position forever is what you should do.[51]

Of course, when it comes to criminal trials the state *could* always gather more evidence: greater resources could be expended on policing; specialist detectives could be flown in; forensic data could be re-checked. But this is true of every case! A guilty or not guilty verdict in a binary system of proof is just a way of saying: 'here is the best judgement we can come up with, given the available evidence'. Court verdicts are always relative to the evidence that has been presented in court; they do not say anything about the completeness of the evidence, nor do they provide a cast-iron guarantee that we should not reopen the inquiry at a later time. Indeed, even if the evidence at one time strongly supports a given conclusion, this doesn't mean that new evidence cannot turn things on their head to support the opposite conclusion instead. Understood properly, there is not anything about an intermediate verdict that makes it 'less final' than classic binary verdicts.

However, there is a different way to push this idea of intermediate verdicts being a problematic 'compromise'. Some studies on the Scottish not proven

---

[51] Consider the religious agnostic!

verdict have suggested that third verdicts serve to draw juries away from guilty verdicts.[52] You can imagine the process as one where one juror proposes to convict, a second juror raises some doubts, and all agree on a third juror's proposal to return a not proven verdict as a way to 'meet in the middle'. We can conjecture that the presence of an intermediate verdict reduces the number of convictions overall.

You can react to this 'compromise' phenomenon in different ways.[53] On the one hand, it could be seen as a good thing to prevent juries or judges from convicting when they are not entirely sure of guilt. Perhaps intermediate verdicts focus the mind by reminding the jury just how confident they should be before finding someone guilty. Indeed, the fact that jurors are split in their individual verdicts might be a good indication that they should collectively agree to 'split the difference' and endorse an intermediate verdict. It indicates that the evidence is not clear-cut in favour of guilt or innocence. On the other hand, it could be seen as a type of cowardice that allows the fact-finder to escape the unpleasant business of sticking their neck out and making a difficult decision. If intermediate verdicts short-circuit proper and full deliberation, then this would be a problem. An intermediate verdict agreed after careful deliberation is defensible; returning an intermediate verdict to escape deliberation is not.

Since empirical work suggests that including intermediate verdicts does reduce the number of convictions, it must also reduce the number of false convictions. But, some worry that this comes at the disproportionate cost of allowing too many guilty people to escape justice. Given the ongoing argument about low rates of conviction for sexual criminality, some have argued that mechanisms which reduce conviction rates are problematic. It *is* true that intermediate verdicts are more common in sexual offences than in other types of offence, something that campaign groups have been keen to highlight. For example, in their campaign against non-binary verdicts, Rape Crisis Scotland points to the fact that 'not proven' acquittals are more than twice as common in rape cases (44 per cent) compared to other offences (20 per cent), along with the fact that rape cases have the lowest conviction rate compared to any crime type.[54] This is a key reason why the Scottish Government seeks to abolish the not proven verdict and return to a binary system. (A similar trend is found in Israel, where 'acquittal on the basis of doubt' is more common in sexual offence cases than in other types of case.[55])

---

[52] See Chalmers, Leverick, and Munro 2022.

[53] Something worth considering is psychological research on 'extremeness aversion', where people tend to prefer – and be biased towards – options that lie between extremes. For a meta-analysis, see Neumann, Böckenholt, and Sinha 2016.

[54] See Rape Crisis Scotland n.d.   [55] Rabin and Vaki 2023.

An assumption at play in this argument is that the 'base rate' of guilty people is much higher than currently reflected in conviction rates for sexual offences – namely, that it is worth making the trade-off of a few more innocent people being convicted in order to convict many more guilty people. Even if this is right, there are further questions we might have about this argument. One, for instance, is whether it is acceptable to remove the safeguard that intermediate verdicts provide in *all* crimes just to make it easier to get convictions in sexual offence trials. Another is whether it is legitimate to make assumptions about what a 'better' conviction rate would be, without being seen to endorse the problematic idea that public authorities should have targets regarding the proportion of convictions.[56]

3.4 Radical Departures from the Binary

We've restricted ourselves to discussing systems where there are only three verdicts, with two being different types of acquittal. However, there are many ways in which legal systems could offer even more precise evaluations about the strength of evidence. In theory, we could have very information-rich systems, where courts return precise probability estimates about the guilt of the accused.[57] There is something dystopian-sounding about this, but it is hard to put a finger on what. We might doubt that humans are especially good at thinking with mathematical precision about probability of guilt. It has a ring of artifice to firmly distinguish evidence supporting a 60 per cent versus a 70 per cent chance of guilt. Perhaps more fundamentally, ternary systems (like 'not proven') are still rooted in a sort of everyday practice; there is nothing unusual about remaining neutral or having an intermediate confidence about something after considering all the evidence. But precise probability estimates depart considerably from the ordinary way in which we evaluate each other. Still, it is worth raising such systems as a possibility, even if only because asking why we don't do things this way sheds light on our philosophical commitments.

Even if systems assigning precise probabilities to guilt are unpalatable, there are various other approaches that attempt to incorporate the idea that we should have a wider menu of possible responses to criminal accusations. For example, take the ternary 'not proven' system. One could suppose that it is appropriate to bar someone with a not proven verdict for sexual assault from certain types of employment, while not barring the same person if they receive a 'full' acquittal. There are many variants here. Federico Picinali, for example, discusses what he

---

[56] See Thomas 2023 for important evidence that suggests that juries are not primarily responsible for the low conviction rate for sexual offences.

[57] For a helpful discussion, see Spottswood 2021.

calls a 'conditional acquittal'. This would involve giving a *harsher* punishment to the person given the conditional acquittal if found guilty at a later date of another offence.

In this provocative vein, I want to close this section with an even more radical way of proportioning the reaction of the court to the evidence: the possibility of graded punishment for the guilty. In everyday life, sometimes the best thing is to proportion our practical reaction to the evidence. For example, sticking with mountain-related examples, think about how weather can affect holiday walking plans. If it's certain to rain, you might call off the trip (no point trudging in the wet and cold). If it's certain to be sunny, you might plan to walk on a particular day (e.g. Saturday – then you can do something different on Sunday, like read legal history). If the weather is less predictable, you might plan to stick around in the area for longer (say, Saturday *and* Sunday) to give you best chance to complete the hike. It's often sensible to change how we act in cases where the evidence isn't decisive, doing something different from what you would do if the evidence were decisive in either direction. So, why not do the same in criminal justice? Why not punish the guilty in proportion to how confident we are in their guilt?

Under the most comprehensive version of a graded punishment system, we would punish most harshly those whom we were 100 per cent confident are guilty, punish slightly less harshly those whom we were only 95 per cent confident were guilty, and so on, continuing to lower the level of punishment as our confidence in guilt decreased. Presumably, there would be some level – some 'blame line' – below which we wouldn't punish at all. (It would be perverse to punish someone we thought was only 1 per cent likely to be guilty!) While at first blush such a system may sound perverse, it is not entirely unmotivated. For example, with any conviction, there is the risk of making a mistake. If a mistake has been made, any retributive punishment is (arguably) immoral, any rehabilitative efforts are wasted, and the public expense of punishment has been for naught. Proportioning the level of punishment to the level of confidence in guilt is a way to hedge our bets.

Even putting aside systems that use very fine-grained confidence levels, there are more coarse-grained alternatives available. Talia Fisher has explained that one might have a system involving multiple guilty verdicts corresponding to different standards of proof.[58] To illustrate, consider:

- Guilt beyond any doubt.
- Guilt beyond a reasonable doubt.
- Guilty on the basis of clear and convincing evidence.

---

[58] Fisher 2021.

One might have a system where each of these receives different treatment: in terms of the duration of formal punishment, availability of appeal, possibility of parole, or severity of the punishment. Indeed, we noted earlier that some think that the death penalty should only be available when the crime is proven beyond *any* doubt. Implementing such a process across the entire criminal justice system would obviously require a radical rethink of criminal justice. I don't defend or advocate for this system, but I leave it as an exercise for the reader to consider what (if anything) is wrong with it. This will clarify your thinking about fundamental questions concerning the purpose of criminal justice and punishment.

4 Legal Probabilism and Anti-Probabilism

Proof is fundamentally about strength of evidence. Evidence makes accusations and claims more or less *likely*, can *explain* why something happened, can lead us to *believe* something or reject it, can render certain doubts *reasonable* or *unreasonable*. We have used this terminology more or less interchangeably so far. Now, I want to ask whether we can be more precise in understanding the relationship between evidence and proof.

4.1 Probabilism and Anti-Probabilism

Consider the following idea:

Legal probabilism: Legal proof is justifying the *probability* of guilt/liability above some threshold.

Probabilism, as the name suggests, views the standards of proof in terms of probabilities.[59] Probabilities are quantitative measurements of how likely something is, on a scale that ranges from 0–1. Something that has a probability of 1 is certain, 0 is certain not to happen, while something that has a probability of 0.5 is just as likely as not to happen. (If you prefer, you can convert these into percentages: e.g. 0.5 = 50 per cent.)

Probabilism seems to offer a pretty compelling diagnosis of the civil standard of proof. What is it to prove something on the 'balance of probabilities'? Well, according to probabilism, it is to show that it is >0.5 likely to be true. Probabilism might seem less obvious when applied to the criminal standard of proof, that is, the BRD test. We might think that deciding whether a doubt is 'reasonable' is not just a matter of estimating the likelihood of error, but something more qualitative in nature. But if what makes a doubt reasonable is

---

[59] See Urbaniak and Di Bello 2021 for general introduction. Hedden and Colyvan 2019 summarise and respond to objections to Probabilism.

not about how likely the accusation is to be wrong, then what else could it be about? The difficulty of answering this question can be used to support probabilism.

We need to distinguish between debates about (i) how the current system works and (ii) how legal systems should be designed. One question is – can we interpret 'beyond reasonable doubt' in a probabilistic way? This question is separable from the larger question – should we implement standards of proof defined explicitly in terms of probabilities? Defining criminal proof in terms of a precise probability (e.g. 0.9 likelihood of guilt) is one way to escape the notorious vagueness that many see in the current BRD standard. Some think the fact that BRD is so hard to define is problematic – after all, shouldn't people know exactly what standard they will be judged against?[60] However, as discussed earlier, the vagueness of the criminal standard can be defended because it empowers the judge or jury to apply standards that are most appropriate to the case at hand.

What I do in this section is to try and make progress in understanding legal proof by articulating and explaining why some hold the opposing view to probabilism:

Legal anti-probabilism: Something cannot be legally proven just by showing that it exceeds some probability threshold.

Anti-probabilism is a negative claim, denying the truth of probabilism. It has been endorsed by a wide range of philosophers working on legal philosophy. On anti-probabilist views, one cannot prove something *simply* by showing that it is very likely. There are many different types of anti-probabilist view which have lots of detail and nuance. However, before looking at these, we should say something about why anyone might be sceptical about probabilism in the first place.

First, it might seem arbitrary to say that someone deserves punishment if their guilt is proven to a 0.95 likelihood but not a 0.94 likelihood. Can this be used as an argument against probabilism?[61] I don't think so. We could use the same argument for a 0.94/0.93 probability and so on right down to 0. But this surely wouldn't be right! There are sharp cut-offs under almost any way we think about proof. Even if we think only in qualitative terms, the difference between a reasonable and an unreasonable doubt will sometimes be determined by small differences in the evidence or psychology of the fact-finder. The probabilistic approach simply makes sharp cut-offs explicit. We also use sharp cut-offs in other

---

[60] For example, see Laudan 2006.

[61] You might reflect on Section 3 on intermediate verdicts and develop this objection.

areas of life (e.g. deciding who gets medical treatment) so it isn't obvious that the existence of sharp boundaries is objectionable when difficult decisions must be made.

Another worry could be that just focusing on probabilities omits other important notions concerning how evidence can support a conclusion. For example, we might be interested in the coherence of evidence or how well corroborated evidence is. Perhaps these notions are hard to capture in purely probabilistic terms? Evaluating this abstract challenge would require spending a long time discussing different ways of interpreting the idea of probability to see if our preferred notion could capture these other evaluative ideas.[62]

Since we are limited for space, I will take a different approach and focus instead on what has been the biggest challenge to probabilism in recent years – a purported type of counterexample. The challenge comes from the 'proof paradox'.

4.2 The Proof Paradox

The proof paradox is generated by cases where a conclusion has strong probabilistic support yet many resist judging the conclusion proven. The cases used to generate the proof paradox involve *statistical evidence* supporting guilt or liability. The idea will be best appreciated by considering influential examples from the literature.[63]

4.2.1 Civil Law

Gatecrasher. The organisers of the local rodeo are suing John for gatecrashing their event. Their evidence is as follows: John attended the Sunday afternoon event– he was seen and photographed there. No tickets were issued, so John cannot be expected to prove he bought a ticket with a ticket stub. However, while 1,000 people were counted in the seats, only 300 paid for admission.[64]

Blue Bus. A bus negligently causes injury to a pedestrian, but it is not known which company the bus belongs to. On the route where the accident occurred, the Blue Bus Company runs 75 per cent of the buses. There is no further information available to settle which company the bus belongs to.[65]

[62] See section 2 of Hedden and Colyvan 2019 for a flavour of how this debate might go.
[63] For a different summary, see Redmayne 2008 or Ross 2020.
[64] Adapted from Blome-Tillmann 2020, 565; original case due to Cohen 1977.
[65] Adapted from Tribe 1971, 1340–1.

4.2.2 Criminal Law

Prisoners. One hundred prisoners are exercising in the prison yard. Ninety-nine of them suddenly join in a planned attack on a prison guard; the hundredth prisoner plays no part. There is no evidence available to show who joined in and who did not.[66]

Riot. An electronics store is struck by looters during a riot. On the day the riot occurs, 100 televisions are taken from the store: the transaction record indicates that only one was purchased legitimately. No receipt was issued. Joel is stopped by the police while carrying a television. Joel concedes he has one of the 100 televisions taken from the store – 99 of which were stolen – but maintains his innocence.[67]

4.2.3 Discussion

While these examples are philosophical inventions there are real legal cases that resemble these stylised scenarios.[68] And, as I later show, there are other cases with huge public significance that are structurally similar.

Many feel uncomfortable about relying on purely statistical evidence to convict someone of a crime or hold them liable for a civil wrong. However, this discomfort is not easy to reconcile with the standards of proof. The civil law provides the clearest illustration. The civil standard of proof is 'the balance of probabilities'. It seems, by stipulation, more likely than not that the Blue Bus caused the accident or that a generic rodeo attendee is more likely a gatecrasher than not. The criminal cases have a less paradoxical flavour – one might think it reasonable to have doubts in both the Riot and Prisoners cases. But why? After all, the probability of guilt is 99 per cent. Surely *other* criminal cases are settled on weaker evidence, evidence that would not support such a high confidence in guilt. For example, there is well-documented evidence on the limitations and unreliability of eyewitnesses in stressful situations.[69] Many eyewitness accounts might not be judged 99 per cent reliable. Yet, absent exculpatory evidence, the evidence of a direct eyewitness is sometimes regarded as sufficient for conviction. So, it remains puzzling why strong statistical evidence cannot perform the same role.[70]

We need to distinguish two questions: the psychological question of how people tend to react to statistical evidence, and the normative question of how the legal system *should* react. There is, I think, a clear psychological difference in how people react to statistical versus more direct types of evidence. Indeed,

---

[66] Adapted from Redmayne 2008, 282–3.   [67] Adapted from Smith 2020, 93.

[68] *Smith* v. *Rapid Transit Inc.* [317 Mass. 469, 58 N.e.2d 754], for instance, resembles the Blue Bus case.

[69] For example, see Loftus 1996.

[70] The focus is on whether it is acceptable to rely on statistical evidence alone to convict or hold someone liable. The debate is not primarily about whether statistical evidence should be admissible, nor whether statistical evidence can be exculpatory.

discomfort about relying on purely statistical evidence is known as the 'Wells effect', after the psychologist – Gary Wells – who published a paper describing it.[71] The question is whether this psychological reaction is an irrational anti-statistical bias or whether it is justified.

Many have tried to vindicate the anti-statistical intuitions generated by the proof paradox. If this can be done, we have a counterexample to probabilism. These discussions have a long history, the proof paradox having been debated intermittently by legal scholars since the mid twentieth century, before being rediscovered more recently by philosophers.[72] I want to start by discussing recent work primarily carried out by philosophers working in epistemology.

4.3 Epistemic Responses to the Proof Paradox

Philosophers have noted that the proof paradox has important similarities with famous epistemological puzzles, most notably puzzles about lotteries.

Some propositions about lotteries are stupendously likely to be true. Consider the proposition 'any given ticket in a ten-million ticket lottery is a losing ticket'. Despite being overwhelmingly likely to be true, many philosophers think that such propositions, based on probabilities alone, are different from other propositions we regularly rely upon.[73] It's been popular to suppose, for instance, that we don't *know* that we have lost the lottery just by reflecting on how unlikely winning is. This is puzzling, because there are *many* things we take ourselves to know even though we presumably have more than a one-in-ten-million chance of being wrong. For example, you might know you will attend a meeting later, even though occasionally meetings get cancelled unexpectedly – and surely more frequently than one-in- ten-million meetings! If we want to avoid conceding that the scope of our knowledge is much more limited than usually supposed, there must be some difference between the probabilistic evidence we have about the lottery and evidence for regular things that we do know.

Something to note about 'lottery beliefs' is that, even though they are very likely to be correct, there is another sense in which they are not secure. They are insecure because the evidence supporting these beliefs is completely compatible with your belief about impending lottery loss being false. Suppose you *did* have the winning ticket. Nothing would be different from your perspective. All the same probabilistic evidence against your victory would remain. Perhaps *non*-statistical evidence provides a tighter or more direct connection with the

---

[71] See Wells 1992.

[72] Classic earlier work on the proof paradox includes Cohen 1977 and Tribe 1971.

[73] See Ebert, Smith, and Durbach 2018 for an empirical study of lottery propositions and philosophical references.

truth? This is an imprecise, inchoate thought. An influential way of responding to the proof paradox tries to develop it.

The general strategy has been to borrow ideas from epistemology about the rationality of belief. The assumption behind this strategy draws on something discussed in Section 1 – that legal verdicts and individual beliefs should be judged against similar standards. Of course, we have already noted that acquittals can be legitimate even if you don't fully believe in the innocence of the accused. Rather, the idea is that *guilty verdicts* should be based on evidence that would make believing in guilt rational. We can put the idea like this:

Legal doxasticism.[74] Guilty verdicts must only be issued when it is rational, given the evidence, to believe that the accused is guilty.

But what are the requirements for a belief to be rational? I will briefly introduce four theories that flesh out this idea.

Sensitivity. A belief is sensitive when it has the following property: it is a belief you would not have had if the belief were false. Some methods tend to produce sensitive beliefs (e.g. using your eyes in good conditions, because the fact you believe an object is there depends on the object being there) while other methods do not produce sensitive beliefs (e.g. predicting the future using tarot cards, because the future isn't determined by the cards you draw). Sensitivity is thus a way to capture the intuitive idea of 'tracking the truth'. Beliefs formed on the basis of statistics alone are not sensitive. Take the lottery case again – if you trust the statistics, you would have formed the same (false) belief about losing even in the event that you had a winning ticket. Some argue that we should only convict people when our belief in their guilt is sensitive – we acquire these beliefs by using methods that track the truth.[75]

Safety. Safety is a property of belief, often informally presented as a belief that couldn't easily have been false. This might sound uninformative, but the idea is usually developed by appealing to the idea that we can rank possibilities (or 'worlds') with respect to how close or far they are from the actual world. In this way, you can compare counterfactual situations against each other in terms of how close a possibility they were – for example, a world where humans are 200 feet tall is further away than a world where it rained yesterday morning. Safe beliefs are beliefs that are true in all nearby worlds. Some claim that beliefs formed on the basis of mere statistics are often unsafe because statistical evidence doesn't show that an incompatible conclusion was counterfactually

---

[74] 'Doxastic' means pertaining to belief.

[75] Sensitivity in epistemology is famously defended by Robert Nozick as a condition on knowledge. See Melchior 2019, chapter 2 for an introduction. It is defended in legal philosophy by (among others) Enoch, Spectre, and Fisher 2012 and Enoch and Spectre 2019.

Philosophy of Law

distant. For example, you might say that winning the lottery is always a close possibility even though statistically unlikely; all that has to happen for you to win is for some balls to drop into a hopper differently. Some argue that we should only convict when our belief that someone is guilty is safe – when the evidence shows that the accused being innocent is only a distant possibility.[76]

Knowledge. Knowledge is widely considered to have deep cognitive and social importance. Although (almost) everyone agrees that knowing something entails that it is true, how to further analyse the nature of knowledge is a topic of perennial debate. (Some of the properties discussed above are candidate requirements for a belief to count as knowledge.) It's usually taken for granted that relying on certain types of statistical evidence – as in the lottery – doesn't provide you with knowledge. One idea, popular in some quarters, is that knowledge provides the 'norm' for various practices: forming beliefs, making assertions, relying on something when deciding how to act. For example, the 'knowledge norm of assertion' dictates that you shouldn't go around telling people something will happen unless you know it will happen. Some have used this type of reasoning about the centrality of knowledge to various practices to argue that knowledge is the 'norm' for criminal conviction – you shouldn't pronounce someone guilty unless you know they are guilty (which you don't when relying only on statistics).[77]

Each of these views faces a common problem. They appear too demanding as conditions for a positive legal verdict. Suppose a court convicts someone after diligently seeking out and weighing the evidence, relying on the latest theories, consulting the most relevant witnesses, after an impeccable police investigation, and with the defence lawyer putting up a robust fight. Alas, it turns out the witnesses got it wrong (suppose they all made an honest mistake) and the person was innocent. Still, courts can only judge on the basis of the evidence they have. There will be cases where it is rational for a court to return a verdict that is (unbeknownst to everyone) false. If all the evidence points towards guilt, then it is rational for a jury to convict. If false verdicts can sometimes be rational, given extremely misleading evidence, none of the aforementioned properties can account for this. You can't know the verdict is false (you can't know anything false). False verdicts can also never be sensitive – if the person is innocent and your belief was sensitive then you wouldn't believe they are guilty. Likewise, safety views also seem too strict. This is because philosophers usually stipulate that the actual

[76] Safety in epistemology is famously defended by Sosa 1999, Williamson 2000, and Pritchard 2009. It is defended in legal philosophy by (among others) Pardo 2018 and Pritchard 2022.

[77] Knowledge conditions in legal philosophy are defended by (among others) Blome-Tillmann 2017, Littlejohn 2020, and Moss 2022.

world – that is, what actually happens – is *at least as near a possibility* as any counterfactual possibility. So, false beliefs can never be safe.

Of course, defenders of these views have various responses to this criticism. For example, one might focus on the *tendency of different methods* to produce beliefs that are safe, sensitive, or known – rather than focusing on whether the individual verdicts have these properties. This would of course require spelling out how good the tendency needs to be to pass muster, as well as an account of how to individuate methods.[78] However, we are limited for space so rather than get into these technicalities I want to forge on to another proposed epistemic condition on conviction.[79]

Normalcy. Normalcy is a type of non-probabilistic justification.[80] Informally, normalcy can be introduced with the idea of something 'calling for special explanation'. Some propositions can be highly improbable while being, in the explanatory sense, entirely normal. Winning the lottery is an example; we don't require a special explanation when someone wins the lottery, regardless of how improbable it may be. However, when an eyewitness says 'I watched her steal the money!', we would typically demand a special explanation upon learning that the eyewitness was mistaken and the accused actually innocent. We would demand a special explanation for why the accused was innocent, given that the eyewitness claimed to see them commit the crime. The normic view deals with proof-paradox cases by pointing out that it would *not* take special explanation for belief based merely on statistical evidence to be false. For example, in the Blue Bus case, it would not take special explanation for it to have been a Red Bus causing the accident – after all, the Red Bus Company runs 25 per cent of the buses on the route.

An advantage of 'normic' theories is that a belief can be justified in the normic sense despite being false. For example, if all the eyewitness evidence seemed to point towards guilt, it *would* require special explanation if it turned out that the accused was innocent. Hence, the false belief in guilt would have normic justification. The normic view seems to escape the 'demandingness' worry afflicting other epistemic diagnoses of the proof paradox.

But the normic view has its own problems.[81] One is about the idea of something requiring special explanation. You might worry that this idea is relative to: (i) how well informed we are about the fallibility of the evidence, and (ii) the way in which the evidence is presented. For example, as our

---

[78] This has proven a notoriously difficult project in epistemology! See Conee and Feldman 1998 for a discussion of how hard it is to individuate methods for forming beliefs.

[79] There are also other epistemic conditions that have been defended as conditions on legal proof. For example, see Gardiner 2019 and Lackey 2021.

[80] Normalcy in defended in epistemology by Smith 2016 and in legal epistemology by Smith 2018.

[81] For further discussion of objections to normic views, see Di Bello 2020.

psychological knowledge grows, the less surprising it becomes for an eyewitness to get things wrong. An expert in psychology might not demand a special explanation for the fallibility of an eyewitness, since they know eyewitnesses get things wrong all the time, especially in stressful situations. Indeed, the expert might know eyewitnesses simply get things wrong x per cent of the time. One day, we might even have eyewitness accounts presented in court in the form of a probabilistic estimate as to how likely they are to be accurate. (Indeed, a deep philosophical question looms – is there any underlying truth about whether evidence is *really* probabilistic or non-probabilistic, or does it rather depend just on the way that the evidence is presented?) What is normically supported might shrink in the face of our advancing knowledge. Yet, it strains our credulity to suppose that we shouldn't convict people if there is both statistical and eyewitness evidence against them – even if neither is normically supported in the eyes of someone who perfectly understands the fallibility of such evidence.

A more general objection to all epistemic accounts is that intuitions about evidence that lacks the aforementioned properties seem less secure when we *combine* different types of probabilistic evidence. Consider the following variation on the Blue Bus case.

> **Blue Bus variation**: A bus causes injury to a pedestrian, but it is not known which company the bus belongs to. On the route where the accident occurred, the Blue Company runs 75 per cent of the buses and the Red Company 25 per cent of the buses. Fresh tyre marks are found at the scene of the accident that an investigator's uncontested report states were caused by the offending vehicle. All parties agree these could only be made by a certain brand of bus tyre. A recent insurance application form shows that 90 per cent of Blue Company buses have the implicated brand of bus tyre, while only 5 per cent of Red Company buses do. Moreover, police find a bus hubcap on the road immediately after the crash. Only 2 per cent of Red Company buses were recorded as having the implicated brand of hubcap, while 96 per cent of Blue Company buses have it.[82]

At the end of the day, the totality of the evidence against the Blue Bus Company remains statistical. Yet, it seems less compelling to suppose that we should not hold them responsible.

4.4 DNA Evidence

I want to discuss a final interesting test case for probabilism – convictions based on 'cold-hit' DNA evidence.[83]

---

[82] Taken from Ross 2021b.
[83] DNA evidence is further discussed in Roth 2010 and Ross 2021a.

Everyone knows that forensic evidence can play an important role in criminal investigations. For instance, DNA evidence is often regarded as a gold standard in linking somebody to an unsolved murder or sexual assault. However, people are generally less familiar with the nature of such evidence and how it is presented in court.

Perhaps surprisingly, DNA evidence is presented in court just as a probabilistic estimate. A forensic expert provides the evidence. But they do not categorically say 'this DNA belongs to that person'. Rather, they make claims like 'the probability of the DNA *not* belonging to that person is one in ten million'. Why do they hedge their bets? Because, for any apparent DNA match, there is the tiny possibility that it is a *random match.* In other words, it is possible for an incriminating sample to *seem to match your DNA* even though you had nothing to do with the crime. Often, this tiny risk is washed out because DNA evidence is usually combined with other evidence linking the accused to the crime. But, in so-called cold-hit cases, such as where new techniques allow recovery of DNA evidence about historic crimes, we might not have any evidence apart from the matching DNA sample.

What should we do if all we have is the DNA match? Courts have struggled to decide whether it is acceptable to convict someone if the only evidence is a matching DNA profile. On the one hand, DNA evidence gives rise to probabilities *much* greater than those found in regular proof-paradox cases, as strong (or stronger than) a one-in-*ten-million* chance of error. Rejecting cold-hit DNA evidence would make for a less accurate criminal justice system. On the other hand, there is something 'lottery like' in DNA profiles, given the possibility of a random match. This means we have an interesting way to test intuitions about the proof paradox and probabilism. The heart of cold-hit DNA evidence is just an incriminating statistic giving rise to a probability estimate of guilt.

Interestingly, this generalises to other types of forensic evidence. There have been attempts to estimate fingerprint matches in probabilistic terms, rather than relying on dubiously reliable qualitative assessments. There can also be improbable random matches between unrelated fingerprint samples, since there is always a tiny statistical chance that two people are born with practically indistinguishable fingerprints.

Pushing the argument further, we might then consider cases involving conjunctions of incriminating forensic evidence and probabilistic evidence.

> **Prisoners and DNA.** One hundred prisoners are exercising in the prison yard. Extremely grainy CCTV footage shows that ninety-nine of them attack and kill the guard. The 100th prisoner played no role in the assault and could have done nothing to stop it. From the footage it is impossible to distinguish which prisoners were involved. The ninety-nine murderers escape in one

direction and, some time later, the 100th prisoner escapes in a different direction. One prisoner is recaptured. Upon testing, it is found that his DNA matches the most dominant DNA profile found on a discarded switch-blade used in the murder. The forensic scientist estimates the chance of a random DNA match as one in ten million.[84]

Here, it seems rather far-fetched to claim that it would be inappropriate to convict. Yet, on one reading, the evidence remains purely statistical. So, perhaps the 'proof-paradox' argument against probabilism isn't so decisive?

4.5 Moral and Political Diagnoses

Some have worried that focusing only on epistemic ideas fails to see the woods for the trees. Enoch, Fisher, and Spectre argue that some legal philosophers are exhibiting a type of 'epistemic fetish' by focusing on epistemic properties rather than the moral–political values that, ultimately, the legal system is intended to promote.[85] If this is right, it would be better to think about these moral or political ends first, then see where the epistemology fits in.

Just as with epistemological diagnoses of the proof paradox, many moral and political approaches take an inchoate thought and try to develop it. The kernel at the heart of many accounts begins from the idea that justice requires treating people as *individuals* and that relying on statistical evidence somehow fails to do this. By assuming that someone is just the same as other members of a reference class (e.g. rodeo attendees, prisoners, rioters) a worry is that we somehow disrespect or degrade the individuality of the person being accused. This inchoate thought seems to chime with what is wrong with statistical evidence in other contexts. For example, another debate concerns demographic profiling – using statistical evidence about racial, ethnic, or gender groups to attribute properties to people.[86] In this debate, many think we somehow treat people badly by lumping them in with other members of their group.

Various accounts try to sharpen this idea. One is that basing legal verdicts on mere statistics *disrespects* the individual, while another is that it fails to show due regard for one's *autonomy* to diverge from one's peers.[87] Others have suggested that ignoring individuality shows that the state is insufficiently concerned with the individual's *right to security* from being harmed by false convictions.[88] Such accounts can then be used to backwards engineer an account of why certain types of evidence – evidence that is somehow

---

[84] Taken from Ross 2021b.   [85] Enoch, Fisher, and Spectre 2021
[86] For example, see Gendler 2011; Bolinger 2020; Ross 2022.
[87] See Levanon 2022 and Wasserman 1992, respectively.   [88] See Adams 2023.

individualised – is morally important. Indeed, perhaps such ideas about the importance of individualised evidence could explain the moral importance of the various epistemic properties discussed earlier.[89]

One immediate issue with this individuality-based approach is that the defending party in the proof paradox need not be an individual at all.[90] As the Blue Bus case shows, the party inculpated by statistics can be a corporation. Indeed, the defending company can be a powerful multinational that has, in all likelihood, harmed a vulnerable individual. It's not obvious that we owe it to such corporations to respect their individuality in a way that rules out using statistical evidence against them. I return to this issue at length shortly.

Diagnoses that appeal to individuality and the importance of individualised evidence focus on what we owe to people, rather than the consequences of relying on statistical evidence. But some reject statistical evidence by reflecting on the effect that relying on such evidence might have.

One concern is that *if* we rely on statistical evidence, we might commit ourselves to a procedure that would guarantee eventually making a mistake.[91] For example, take the Gatecrasher case. If we decided the evidence was strong enough to sanction one person, then by parity of reasoning it would be strong enough to sanction everyone at the rodeo. But then we would be sure to sanction a large number of innocent people, which seems patently unjust. However, while an important point, this cannot be a *general* diagnosis of the proof paradox. In some cases – like the Blue Bus or DNA cases – we don't have any certainty that relying on statistics about a given incident would guarantee a mistake, nor are a large group of people put 'on the hook' by relying on statistics.

David Enoch, Levi Spectre, and Talia Fisher have argued that relying on bare statistics is no good given the *incentive structure* we want the law to create. Obviously, we want people to follow the law – and we want evidence law to give people an incentive to follow the law by making sure that, if they break the law, there will likely be admissible evidence that can be used against them. Perhaps relying on statistics can create perverse incentives? In some cases it might. For example, consider the decision-making of someone wondering whether to buy a ticket in the Gatecrasher case described earlier (recall: no record will be provided of their purchase). If they know that statistical evidence is enough to find them liable, then whether or not they purchase a ticket will make no difference to the inculpatory evidence against them. If we have a general principle that inculpatory evidence should be created by one's choices and

---

[89] For discussion, see Mortini 2022.   [90] This point is also made by Pundik 2008.
[91] For example, see Nunn 2015.

actions, then this is a mark against purely statistical evidence which remains inculpatory pretty much independently of what an individual chooses to do.[92]

A worry with this story about incentives, however, concerns whether it is supposed to be an empirical claim or just a theoretical one. Empirically, it isn't clear that proof-paradoxical cases are common enough to really have any substantial effect on the incentives created by the law. For example, do we really think that the mere possibility of Blue Bus-style cases influences a transportation company CEO? Perhaps the worry is more theoretical rather than practical. But, it isn't clear why this theoretical worry matters so much.

To explain why, I want to draw attention to an under-emphasised side of the debate: the moral problems with *refusing* to rely on statistical evidence. The existence of these moral issues not only casts doubt on the idea that relying on statistics is always wrong, but also calls into question whether it is sensible to look for a single general response that aims to capture every case of purely statistical evidence.

4.6 The Cost of Denying Statistics

Classic 'proof-paradox' cases direct us to focus on the possibility of punishing the wrong person. However, this obscures the fact that refusing to rely on statistical evidence can be to the extreme detriment of the person *harmed*. Proof-paradox scenarios involve an 'epistemic gap' – a situation where we lack the knowledge needed to identify the party responsible for a harm we know has been wrongfully caused. Take the Blue Bus case. Something easy to overlook is that, if we *don't* rely on statistical evidence, we might leave a person who has been negligently squashed without compensation. These issues become sharper in cases where the probability of error is very small and where there is an economic imbalance between the harmed party and putative wrongdoer. For example, consider the following variant on the Blue Bus case.

> **Monopoly Bus**: A bus negligently causes injury to a pedestrian, who is left with life-changing injuries and unable to work. But there was no eyewitness evidence linking the bus to a particular company. On the route where the accident occurred, only one outfit has a regular service: the Monopoly Bus Company. Uncontested statistics from analysing CCTV cameras in adjacent neighbourhoods show that only 1 in every 10,000 buses passing through that area is owned by a private individual. There is no further information.[93]

---

[92] Indeed, as Enoch et al. (2012) point out, this is a mark in favour of methods that produce *sensitive* verdicts – because sensitive methods are sensitive to individual choices and actions.

[93] Ross 2021c, 326.

The evidence remains statistical, but I feel no reluctance about relying on it. This shows that our judgements are sensitive to the relative position of the parties and various justice-related factors – not just to the epistemic properties of the evidence. Indeed, I think that this suggests that there is not necessarily anything paradoxical about (many) so-called proof-paradox cases. Sometimes we should rely on statistical evidence when doing so is to the benefit of the least well off.

One might complain that these cases are philosophical inventions or so rare as to be irrelevant to real legal practice. The complaint would be mistaken. Structurally similar issues have arisen in some of the most controversial legal cases, particularly in 'tort' law. Tort law is the branch of law that provides compensation for negligently caused harms, where being negligent does not reach the standard needed for something to count as a criminal matter. For example, if a shopkeeper's sign is sloppily installed and hits you on the head, this may be a tort that you are entitled to be compensated for.

A normal requirement in tort law is that the person who is harmed shows that the other party *caused* the harm. For example, you might be asked to prove that the shopkeeper hung the sign, and their shoddy handiwork is the reason that it fell on your head. Causation can be easier or harder to prove depending on the case. But sometimes it is nigh impossible.

Litigation about asbestos is one important example.[94] As is well known, and known long before it was effectively regulated, asbestos causes serious and sometimes fatal damage to the human respiratory system. Industrial labourers – and their partners who cleaned their asbestos-caked clothes – got seriously ill and in many cases died premature deaths from asbestos exposure. This was typically because employers failed to take reasonable steps to protect workers from exposure, such as by providing adequate safety equipment. However, labourers often handled asbestos while working for many different employers during their lives. How could they prove that their illness was caused by any *particular* employer? Many of their employers were negligent (by failing to provide safety equipment) but none could be shown to be responsible for any particular illness. Just think about the impossibility of tracing the influence of some asbestos fibres on a disease and demonstrating that these fibres entered the body during one period of employment rather than another.

The way causation is usually understood in the law is through a 'but for test'. In other words, you ask 'but for x, would y have happened?'. If the answer is no, then x is said to have caused y. In asbestos cases, however, it was impossible to

---

[94] I discuss this at length in Ross 2021c. Another important example is the doctrine of market-share liability. For additional discussion, see Krauss 2020.

show that the disease wouldn't have happened but for the time the labourer spent working at any particular company. Yet, clearly all of the employers were at fault. Given that these labourers and their partners were sometimes suffering fatal illness due to employer negligence, it would clearly be a massive injustice if they were unable to gain compensation.

In such cases, relying on statistics is all the court can do. The only evidence the labourers could cite was statistical information about the estimated level of exposure each employer had been responsible for and epidemiological statistics about how likely a generic person was to contract a disease given a particular level of exposure. Framed this way, we see that the labourers were being forced to play a potentially fatal lottery by their employers. The courts took the view that such statistical evidence *could* suffice to assign liability to the employers for the diseases.[95] The general approach of holding the employers liable based on statistics seems right to me. In cases such as this, there is a strong case for thinking that any intuitive discomfort we have about relying on statistics is outweighed by imperatives of justice.

Beyond the fact that relying on statistics could remedy an injustice, are there deeper principles that justify using them in such cases? I think so. In the asbestos case, all the employers exhibited similar failings. Even if one employer was 'lucky' in that they didn't actually cause the disease, they were equally blame-worthy as the similarly negligent employer that was 'unlucky' in causing the disease. One might prefer that liability is shared between parties in virtue of their failings, rather than distributed by the vagaries of chance. For example, consider the following principle:

Shared standards: Whenever a harm is negligently caused but falls into an epistemic gap, it is reasonable to apportion responsibility among potential harmers where they share similar standards when conducting the risky activity.[96]

This principle captures the idea that liability should follow negligent behaviour rather than the purely chance matter of whether the negligence actually causes harm.

Now, here is the even more controversial part. If we accept such a principle, then there may be situations where it is similarly justified to use statistics to attribute liability *even in the regular Blue Bus case*. After all, if the companies

---

[95] See *Fairchild* v. *Glenhaven Funeral Services* [2002] UKHL 22 16; *Barker* v. *Corus* [2006] 2 A. C. 572 17; *Sienkiewicz* v. *Greif* [2011] UKSC 10. There are different ways to apportion liability: one is to 'share' full liability, another is to make the parties each 'part' liable in proportion to the risk they have caused.

[96] Taken from Ross 2021c, 327.

each have similar standards, then they are each imposing risks on the public. And such corporations will generally be better able to bear the burden of financial loss as a cost of business compared to the individual who will go without compensation if denied the use of statistical evidence. The Blue Bus case is supposed to be one of the clearest examples of a case where we should not rely on statistics alone. But, once we take into account the different moral considerations, it is not altogether obvious that the traditional reaction to this case is correct.

4.7 Statistics in Criminal Law Reconsidered

I have defended the use of statistics to fill epistemic gaps in the civil law, when using statistics averts serious injustice. This, to my mind, is evidence that we cannot reject probabilism across the board. But does similar reasoning apply to the criminal law?

Recall something we noted in passing when discussing DNA evidence. Rejecting statistical evidence can require that we accept accuracy sacrifices in the legal system. If we refuse to rely on cold-hit DNA evidence, we release people who are *overwhelmingly* likely to be guilty. Echoing the discussion of Larry Laudan in Section 1, recall that if we fail to convict the guilty, this might mean that more crimes are committed as a result. Enoch, Fisher, and Spectre use this observation to pose the provocative question: 'How many more people are you willing to have assaulted, or murdered, or raped under your designed system, just in order to secure [some epistemic status] for the findings of your criminal justice system?'[97]

For example, imposing a 'sensitivity' requirement on guilty verdicts would (arguably) mean we can't convict some apparent sexual offenders on the basis of cold-hit DNA evidence, even though the likelihood of guilt is stupendously high. But why should a legal system do anything other than try to be as accurate as possible? What do we gain by caring about knowledge or other epistemic properties? The sharpest way to put the worry is: why should we willingly be *less* accurate, just in order to promote knowledge, sensitivity, safety, or normalcy?

This is a difficult question! My own answer would return to the idea outlined in Section 1 about the centrality of belief to findings of criminal guilt.[98] Criminal law, as we have discussed, is distinctive compared to civil law; findings of criminal guilt lead to moral blame and the possibility of retributive punishment. It is important that guilty verdicts are based on the sort of evidence that can lead to members of the community believing the person is guilty.

---

[97] Enoch, Fisher, and Spectre 2021, 89–90.   [98] Also, see Ross 2023a.

Aiming to convict only on the basis of evidence that makes it rational to believe something is the best way to make sure this happens. Statistical evidence often fails to generate a full belief; rather, it just elicits a probabilistic estimate. So, there is a natural argument for why courts might refuse to rely on mere statistics – mere statistics don't tend to support a full belief in guilt in the mind of the community. Still, this argument might not rule out statistics in every case. Perhaps DNA evidence, involving such tiny chances of error, does tend to elicit full belief in the guilt of the accused (compared to regular proof-paradox cases involving much shorter odds).

My general view is that discussions of the proof paradox should look at the details of the case at hand. There may be no single resolution to the question of whether we should rely on statistical evidence alone; rather, there will be some cases where it is acceptable and others where it is not. Whether we should be probabilists or anti-probabilists is a case-dependent matter and must be approached by looking at contextual considerations of justice and policy.

5 Who Should Decide?

We now turn to our final question: *who* should decide the outcome of a trial? What person or group should be trusted with deciding whether the standards of proof have been met, thus determining whether the accused is guilty or not?[99]

In some periods of history, communities seemed to leave the decision to God. 'Trial by combat' (letting the disputants fight it out) and 'trial by ordeal' (having the accused perform some risky or wounding task) were both seen as ways as testing the sincerity – the 'oath' – of those accused of wrongdoing. If their oath was good, according to the official story, God would intervene to ensure that they prevailed.[100]

But even in these times, communities were not content to entirely separate proof from the available evidence. Trial by ordeal, for example, was often ambiguous. One ordeal was to pluck a stone from a cauldron of boiling water. If the inevitable wound healed cleanly, it was a sign of innocence; if it festered, it was a sign of guilt. But determining whether a wound is on its way to healing cleanly is a matter of interpretation – one that must be made by humans, even those claiming to interpret on behalf of a supernatural entity. Given what local people knew about the evidence, this would influence their decision.

Legal systems today answer the 'who should decide' question in strikingly different ways. Some leave the decision entirely in the hands of a professional judge who makes judging their career. Others continue the now ancient practice

---

[99] Jurors are also occasionally used in civil trials, for example in assessing defamation cases.
[100] For example, see Baker 2019.

of using a jury of randomly selected members of the community, outsiders who are not members of the legal profession. And others still adopt hybrid models, using a mix of professional and 'lay' members when adjudicating. The way in which legal systems decide trials is often as much a matter of historical circumstance as conscious design. The choice about 'who should decide' raises fundamental philosophical questions about expertise, democracy, and the limits of state power.

This section focuses on assessing trial by *jury* as a way of understanding what is at stake when choosing who decides the outcome of a trial. Of course, our real interest in the jury is *comparative* – whether juries are better or worse than other ways of deciding the results of trials. The main competition (if we suppose that God is not to be disturbed) is trial by professional judge.

5.1 Reliability versus Moral–Political Value

I want to introduce a rough distinction between two criteria against which you can evaluate mechanisms for deciding trials:

(i) How morally or politically valuable the mechanism is.
(ii) How accurate/reliable the mechanism is.

Accuracy – correctly identifying the guilty and the innocent – is obviously of immense importance. But it isn't the only thing that matters. Juries might have value independently of their reliability. For instance, using juries might be defended on political grounds even if they happened to be a bit less reliable than using a professional judge (in the same way as selecting political leaders through election is probably defensible on political grounds *even if* it would be more reliable to have a panel of benign technocrats appoint public officials).

Although juries can have moral–political value beyond accuracy, there is clearly a close relationship between the two values. It is a moral and political problem when trial decision-making is inaccurate. Why? Well, one type of inaccuracy is saying that an innocent person is guilty. Such mistakes lead to an innocent person being wrongfully condemned and punished. It is also morally and politically problematic if a jury decides to acquit a guilty person. For one thing, this type of mistake often leads to the release of someone who might do further harm. Moreover, many think that states have an obligation to punish the guilty. So, irrespective of what *other* strengths trial by jury may have, there is presumably some threshold of accuracy juries must cross in order for them to be acceptable. An argument for the political value of juries would not convince the sceptic if it turned out that juries were creating miscarriages of justice on a massive scale. Accuracy is among the most important moral–political values that a mechanism for deciding trials can have, even though it is not the only one.

Before moving on to what I think are the most convincing arguments for the jury, I want to mention some interesting *moral and political* defences of juries that I do not find fully convincing. One idea is that serving on a jury is character-enhancing. The idea that civic participation is good for us has a long pedigree. John Stuart Mill, for example, argued that providing people with power and responsibility for public decisions develops their faculties and cultivates a sense of appreciation for the public interest.[101] Whether jury service does improve character in this way is ultimately an empirical question. However, given that serving on a jury is something that people do very infrequently, it's unlikely that these character-enhancing benefits (if they exist) alone justify juries – rather, they will be a happy bonus, if juries are justified on other grounds.

Another idea often mentioned is that the jury serves as a type of *symbol*. For example, perhaps the jury is symbolic of democracy or of the importance of the community. While this is a common thought, I am not sure focusing on symbolism alone is a promising way to go. What matters is whether the jury actually *is* democratic or whether it *does* involve the community in the right way, not whether it is a symbol for these things. If juries are not justified on other grounds, then perhaps we should rethink our symbolic attachment to them?[102]

One concrete way the symbolic role of juries could matter is to bolster the perceived link between criminal justice and the interests of the community. Professional judges are often seen as members of the institutional firmament, representing the state or those with power, rather than representing the community. (In some jurisdictions the horsehair wig remains a common sight.) The presence of the jury as a community representative could make a positive difference in how the accused or the victim experiences the case. If the jury does change the experience of the accused, helping them see their blame as rooted in their community, this would be morally significant. However, there are some problems with this suggestion. First, juries are clearly subordinate to the judge during the trial. Second, juries typically play no role in deciding what punishment should follow conviction. If juries are really meant to significantly change the experience of the accused or the victim, we may need to enhance their role.

I also want to mention a few interesting arguments concerning the *accuracy or reliability* of juries that I don't think are decisive either. There are various philosophical arguments for thinking that larger groups tend to be more reliable than smaller groups. This could be one reason to prefer using a group of jurors

---

[101] Mill 2010.　　[102] See Brennan and Jaworski 2015 for discussion of semiotic arguments.

rather than a professional judge. According to a famous proof due to the French mathematician Marquis de Condorcet – 'Condorcet's jury theorem' – groups can become more accurate simply by increasing the number of people that are in them, provided that certain conditions apply. One of these conditions is assuming that the average person is better than a coin flip (i.e. better than random) at getting the right answer.[103]

It may be plausible to think that the average person is better than random at working out whether a witness is telling the truth, since detecting dishonesty is a skill we practice during the course of our normal lives. So perhaps it is reasonable to think that the average person is better than a coin flip at working out whether someone is guilty of a crime or not. However, where Condorcet's jury theorem falls down is in the fact that jurors are not like coin flips. Another condition required for the jury theorem to hold is that the group members cast their vote independently. But trial juries make decisions by collectively debating and discussing the case. Even if the average juror is initially better than chance at getting the right answer, this doesn't prevent a charismatic or stubborn juror with the wrong view from infecting the group. Given that many jury systems require unanimity or near unanimity for conviction, this can be a fatal problem to the idea that juries are reliable just because their average member tends to be reliable.[104]

Another argument is that intellectual diversity – rather than size – can make a group more reliable.[105] Having different people in a group provides a larger number of perspectives and ideas than any individual would have alone. Some claim that this diversity can be even more important than cognitive ability – that diversity can 'make up for' shortcomings in ability. Professional judges often decide cases alone and the judiciary is not particularly diverse; judges are overwhelmingly middle class, from the same ethnicity, and educated at the same institutions. Perhaps the mere diversity of juries makes them better at making decisions? This is hard to assess. While the idea of diversity being epistemically beneficial has some plausibility, it isn't universally true that diversity beats ability. Diversity doesn't help much for topics that are technical or require specific knowledge or experience; for example, two professors of nuclear physics will outperform even 10,000 members of the public in answering questions about nuclear physics. But, technical crimes like fraud aside, many trials concern people's motivations and likely behaviour. Perhaps these are questions where having different ordinary perspectives is helpful?

---

[103] For a very brief introduction, see Siscoe 2022.

[104] See Hedden 2017 for a discussion of possible solutions.

[105] For example, Landemore 2013 has defended this argument for random selection of representatives.

Regardless of whether this argument is plausible, it is not really an argument for using members of the public rather than a *group* of professional judges (and diversifying the judiciary). To be sure, juries are cheaper than having a large staff of professional judges. Nevertheless, economy is not really a satisfying vindication of the jury system. I want to investigate whether there is a deeper reason for involving the public.

5.2 Questions of Law versus Questions of Fact

Let's continue to think about the skills needed to make legal decisions. To do this, we can try and separate different types of questions that arise during a trial. One basic distinction often made by lawyers is between *questions of law* and *questions of fact*.

Questions of law are technical issues about 'what the law is'. This includes substantive law that regulates our conduct outside the courtroom and procedural law that regulates what happens during a trial. Let's focus on an example – the crime of murder. The legal definition of murder is a matter of law. Depending on where you are, the definition will be found in legislation, or a written judgement made by a judge or other respected source. This definition tells us what needs to be proven – in schematic terms – to convict someone of murder. To take the jurisdiction where I studied law, Scotland, the classic definition of murder is 'a wilful act causing the destruction of life'.[106] Law also regulates what evidence can prove that someone committed a murder. A confession obtained through torture is not admissible, for example. Various legal questions about the definition of wrongs and what is required to prove something arise during trials. Some of these questions can be extremely complex, requiring knowledge of technical legal matters. While murder might seem like a common-sense concept, some areas of the law – like fraud, tax, or shipping law – are such that even understanding the relevant laws and concepts takes considerable training and experience.

A common view is that questions of law are best left to a professional judge. After all, the person on the street will not tend to know the precise definition of different legal concepts, where to find these definitions, or how to resolve difficulties in interpreting the law.

Questions of fact – so the traditional story goes – are rather different. Questions of fact roughly concern 'what happened'. During a trial, we need to work out whether certain things happened in the real world before we can apply the law. To return to murder – in order to apply the law of murder correctly, we need to know whether certain alleged facts are true or not. For example, suppose

---

[106] McDonald 1948, 89.

Harry is found dead. To know whether this was murder, we might need to decide whether Sally stabbed Harry or whether Harry just had an unfortunate accident. The role of settling these factual questions is called being the 'fact-finder' in a legal trial. In trials with a jury, the jury is the fact-finder – they decide whether the conditions for legal proof have been met by applying the standard of proof (beyond reasonable doubt) to the factual claims made during the trial.

Answering many 'real-world' questions does not require legal expertise. Professional judges might be legal experts, but they aren't experts on everyday factual questions. Someone with a law degree (attainment of which requires reading textbooks, drinking a lot of coffee, and sitting legal exams) is not taught how to work out whether someone was carrying a knife or held a grudge. Rather, these are questions that anybody can try to answer once they have considered the evidence. Using a jury of a dozen people, you might think, is a reasonable way of harnessing the power we all have to tell apart the plausible from the implausible.

Unfortunately, a neat distinction between strictly legal and strictly factual questions is hard to maintain. This is because fact-finders in trials are routinely asked to make decisions that are not straightforwardly factual. As discussed in Section 1, criminality requires both an action (*actus reus*) and a mental state (*mens rea*). In a criminal murder trial, the fact-finder might have to answer the following question:

Actus Reus: Did the accused shoot and kill the victim?

This is often straightforwardly factual – either x shot y or not; y either died or lived.

But when it comes to the *mens rea*, things aren't so easy. Simply being *causally* responsible for somebody's death is not sufficient to be guilty of murder (after all, perhaps x was an actor and reasonably assumed the gun was loaded with blanks, or maybe x was hallucinating because they had been unwittingly drugged). To be criminal, you must also have a blameworthy mental state. One classic *mens rea* for murder is:

Mens Rea 1: Did the accused *intend* to kill?

Perhaps intention is also a broadly factual question – one about the psychology of the accused. Either x intended to kill or not. Whether this is a merely factual question is, I think, less straightforward.

Still, most jurisdictions have a second *mens rea*, different from intention, yet still regarded as sufficiently blameworthy to be criminalised. For example, someone might deliberately shoot someone in the heat of the moment without ever thinking about whether they might kill them. Here is a second *mens rea* for murder:

Mens Rea 2: Was the accused *reckless* as to the consequences, not caring whether the victim lived or died?

Deciding whether someone is 'reckless' is not like deciding whether they pulled a trigger. Making a judgement about recklessness is an inescapably normative choice. You are deciding not just what happened, but also about the norms or expectations that we should impose on our fellow citizens. For instance, suppose somebody causes death by throwing a single punch in a bar fight, by purposefully shoving someone onto a cycle lane, or by hitting a golf ball at them from a great distance. Are any of these a reckless attitude sufficient for murder? Are all of them? This isn't a straightforwardly factual question. Indeed, there are various other examples in criminal law of this type of 'normative' fact-finding. For example, juries also have to decide whether force used in self-defence is 'proportionate' to the threat. Again, this is not a merely factual question but rather one about the norms we expect our fellow humans to uphold. Normative fact-finding appears in the civil law too. For example, various civil cases depend on working out whether one party has been 'negligent' or 'unreasonable', terms that are clearly normatively loaded.

John Gardner has a nice way of describing the legal role of these evaluative terms.[107] Gardner calls terms like *reckless* or *unreasonable* 'all purpose buck-passers'. It would be impossible, Gardner suggests, for the law to specify *all* the conditions under which someone is reckless or unreasonable. The list would simply run forever, given the dizzying number of ways that humans can behave. Rather, we need to work out whether someone was reckless or unreasonable in conjunction with looking at the specific details of each case. Normative terms like 'reckless', Gardner suggests, passes responsibility ('the buck') for making such decisions to the fact-finder and away from the formal law, thus allowing us to avoid the impossible task of specifying in advance all the types of behaviour that count as reckless or unreasonable.

But, of course, this doesn't (yet) provide any argument for the use of juries. After all, the fact-finder we pass the buck to could just as well be a judge as a jury. We have found that the simple story about judges (as legal experts) only deciding legal questions and the jury (as people with experience in everyday factual questions) only deciding factual questions doesn't quite work. But now we are left asking: why should we leave normative choices – about recklessness, reasonableness, negligence, and so on – to a jury rather than a judge?

---

[107] See Gardner 2015.

5.3 The Democratic Jury?

One attempt at answering this question might appeal to the idea, often heard, that juries are a democratic way of making decisions.[108] While the argument that juries are democratic is common, it is not obvious what this means. After all, in a democratic *state*, laws are passed through the consent of citizens in general.[109] The democratic mandate of lawmakers, ideally, is derived from the entire citizenship – usually millions of people. It's a very non-standard type of democracy where we take laws that have been passed with the mandate of many millions and make their application subject to a further small-scale democracy that depends on the views of only a dozen jurors!

It is true that we should hope that criminal laws enjoy the democratic support of the community. However, even if the criminal law *does* enjoy democratic support in general, we should bear in mind the point we just made. Namely, it is not possible for the law to codify in advance *all* of the situations in which someone is in breach of the law. For example, it is not possible to write down every single situation in which someone is so reckless for it to be fair to charge them with murder (rather than with a lesser offence). This is true even if the law against murder enjoys general democratic support. So, perhaps the democratic argument for the jury is that when we arrive at one of these 'indeterminate' cases, where the law has not specified exactly what should happen, we should leave it to the community to decide how the law should be applied. It is obviously unfeasible to have a referendum every time such a case occurs, so the next best thing is to rely on a citizen jury in the hope of reaching a representative decision. This is one way to understand the claim that juries are democratic – they aim to ensure that laws are applied in line with the 'conscience of the community'.[110] More accurately, most jury systems are not democratic in the regular 'majoritarian' sense. Rather, in many jurisdictions, there are rules that require a jury to be unanimous (or near enough) before convicting someone. So, the jury, even if democratic in the sense of representing community opinion, is skewed towards making sure that people aren't convicted *against* the conscience of the community. This is in line with the characteristic focus of criminal justice that prioritises protecting the accused from wrongful conviction.

---

[108] For discussion of this idea, see Abramson 1993.

[109] Although common law countries complicate this picture since some aspects of law result from judicial decisions rather than legislative bodies.

[110] See Lee 2018 on different ways to interpret this idea, particularly on whether the juror should decide according to their own conscience or on what they think the values of their community are.

To sum up. The idea of the jury as a democratic institution is viable, but only after considering some intricate problems in legal philosophy. Whether this is enough to fully justify the jury is not yet clear. To deepen the argument for juries, I now turn to another way the jury might be said to be the conscience of the community.

5.4 Jury Nullification

Here's a question. What happens if the jury decides to acquit someone for reasons other than the evidence they have heard in court? Answer: nothing. They simply announce their decision and the trial ends. Jury decisions are final.[111] Since the jury does not have to justify their decision (and because they deliberate in secret) they are not answerable for the reasons behind it.[112] Their reasons could be entirely idiosyncratic. Perhaps surprisingly, this deep lack of transparency and accountability could be a *strength* of the jury. This is due to the phenomenon of 'jury nullification', where juries decide based on their own sense of what is right rather than only by attending to the evidence introduced in court.[113]

In Anglo-American legal systems, the power of the jury to nullify trials emerged centuries ago, partly in response to censorious prosecutions. Famous cases involve the jury refusing to convict when the law was being used to trample freedom of religious assembly and freedom of expression.[114] In *Bushel's Case*, the judge ordered the jury to convict a Quaker man for public preaching. Factually, it was clear that the person had been preaching in public. Yet, the jury refused to convict on grounds of conscience. The judge responded by making the following order against the morally squeamish jurors: 'You shall be locked up, without meat, drink, fire, and tobacco; you shall not think thus to abuse the court; we will have a [guilty] verdict by the help of God, or you shall starve for it.' The foreman of the jury appealed, and English law eventually did away with the idea that the judge was entitled to command and censure the jury. Legal historians debate whether these cases support the *legal right* of the jury to nullify in the modern age. But this is merely an academic debate – juries certainly have the

---

[111] Of course, cases can be appealed, but typically only on matters of law rather than on the jury's assessment of the facts.

[112] This discussion focuses on common law jurisdictions. Some jurisdictions in the Civil tradition use verdicts accompanied by some type of reasoning. See Burd and Hans 2018 for discussion.

[113] See also Brooks 2004.

[114] See *Bushel's Case* (1670) 124 E.R. 1006 and the trial of John Peter Zenger, respectively (for information on the latter, see the Encyclopaedia Britannica entry: www.britannica.com/biog raphy/John-Peter-Zenger).

power to nullify trials by refusing to convict the accused irrespective of what the facts are.[115]

Indeed, legal history has numerous examples of juries ameliorating overly harsh legal codes. The death penalty was mandatory for a wide variety of crimes in English medieval common law. There were some ways to escape this sentence, with one being to 'plead the belly' – to claim to be pregnant. If the pregnancy claim was contested, it would be considered by a jury of women, the 'jury of matrons'.[116] Legal historians describe these matrons as a frequently sympathetic bunch, declaring pregnancy even when there was no such baby (a 'pious perjury') to spare the accused from the excessive rigours of capital medieval criminal law. Arguably, jury nullification is deeply woven into the history of criminal law. The question is whether we still need it now, if we grant that today's law is more humane and democratic.

There are at least three types of nullification. One is for juries to block the application of *laws they believe to be unjust* (e.g. the jury thinks that certain narcotics laws are unfair). Second, the jury can block the *unjust application* of a law they believe to be otherwise just. One example might be laws of criminal damage applied to scenarios of civil disobedience. In 2021, members of the environmental protest group 'Extinction Rebellion' were acquitted of criminal damage against the London headquarters of the petroleum company Shell.[117] The evidence was overwhelming. But, clearly, the jury did not want them punished for their consciousness-raising environmental protests. Third, juries can nullify not because they disagree with a law or its application to a particular case, but because they *disagree with the type of punishment* the accused is likely to suffer if found guilty. For example, a jury might decline to convict because they think the punishments for unlawful abortions are currently too harsh (despite agreeing that *some* penalty is appropriate).

Taking a larger view, the power of the jury to nullify trials can be viewed as a protection against state oppression. On the presumption that judges – paid employees of a state institution who can face professional repercussions or even removal – are less likely to nullify unjust laws, this can be seen as an argument for the jury. Jurors only serve temporarily, so they are not concerned about professional reprisals that may result from their decision to nullify in a given case.

Of course, jury nullification is double-edged. A jury that can make a choice for morally admirable reasons can also make a choice for morally bad reasons too. The same secrecy that preserves the ability of juries to counteract

---

[115] Here, I won't talk about the (less discussed) converse case – where a jury finds someone *guilty* despite not thinking the evidence satisfies the standard of proof.

[116] For discussion, see Butler 2019.   [117] For comment, see McConnell 2021.

oppression and immoral criminalisation also enables it to make morally repugnant choices. For example, a jury might acquit someone of a racist crime because the jury itself has racist members. Indeed, this is something that bedevilled attempts to bring racist criminality to justice in Jim Crow-era America.

When assessing nullification, it's important to separate two different questions – (i) should jurors use the power to nullify, if they have it, versus (ii) should the law prevent jurors from nullifying or facilitate it? Whether jurors should nullify unjust laws (if they can) is a question of moral philosophy.[118] Even if the answer in some cases is 'yes' – as it probably is – this does not mean that the state should support or facilitate nullification as a practice. (Consider an analogy. Whether an individual should use a firearm against a violent attacker is a question of moral philosophy. But even if the answer is 'yes', it still might be incumbent on the state to remove the right to bear arms.)

One point in favour of allowing nullification is that there may not be non-oppressive ways to prevent it. Perhaps an official could sit in the deliberation room to ensure juries do not rely on extra-evidential considerations, or the judge could refuse to put the case to the jury if they believe that the evidence is utterly decisive. But these would be controversial measures. Arguably, the power of the jury to nullify might be an unavoidable consequence of a jury system free from state interference. Whether states should go further than permitting the current grey zone around nullification – by, for example, instructing juries about their power to nullify, or entrenching it as a legally recognised right – is a more delicate question. Currently, acquittals due to jury nullification are not differentiated from other types of acquittal. This is arguably a drawback, since no signal is sent to the state about the extent to which prosecutions are failing due to the fact that people disagree with their laws. If we think back to the earlier section on non-binary verdicts (Section 3.1), you might wonder whether having additional verdicts that explicitly involve a declaration of nullification is a good idea.

5.5 Bias, Rape, and 'Jury Science'

There are various other abstract arguments for and against the jury that we might consider. But it is also natural to ask whether we have strong *empirical* evidence about how juries tend to perform and whether we should generally trust their judgement.

We have returned time and again to the worry about a 'justice gap' in sexual offence cases. In England and Wales, it has been claimed that under 2 per cent of

---

[118] See Huemer 2018 for discussion.

rape allegations terminate in a criminal conviction.[119] There has been a lot of debate about why this is. Some of the problems occur pre-trial: for example, in mishandling of complaints by the police. Another issue is that rape is prosecuted less than other crimes, partly because securing knock-down evidence can be more difficult given the typically private nature of the crime. But one possibility – and this is only a possibility – is that juries mistakenly tend to convict less often than a judge would.[120] There are different reasons why this might be. One is that juries just tend to be more credulous and tend to believe the accused more often.[121] Another is that juries tend to take a view different to judges about consent and when belief in consent is reasonable. But most important for our purposes is the possibility that jurors tend to be afflicted by various *biases* that lead their reasoning astray when considering sexual allegations.[122]

This last possibility is especially worrying for the credibility of jury trials. Most of us probably think that some people in our community have various biases and prejudices. Juries are a sample of people in the community. So, we should expect some jury members to have biases and prejudices. This seems like a reasonable argument. Indeed, some have even argued that the threat of prevalent 'rape myths' among jurors is so great as to justify doing away with juries in trials about sexual criminality, even if we retain juries more generally.[123] Of course, an immediate question is whether legal professionals are any different in their vulnerability to bias. However, as a professional group susceptible to selection and training, one *might* hope that it is easier to fight bias in professional judges rather than in a random sampling of the community.

This worry about sexual biases is just one example of a range of worries about whether jurors tend to make the right decision. Here is a fuller list of such worries:[124]

(I) Jury decisions are influenced by interpersonal biases, most prominently:

- racial bias against out-groups/in favour of in-groups
- gendered biases – for example, associating gender with criminality; misogynistic myths about sexual consent
- socio-economic biases – for example, associating 'class' with criminality

---

[119] See HM Government 2021, 7.

[120] However, see Thomas 2023 for empirical analysis suggesting that jurors do not have markedly low conviction rates for various sexual offences.

[121] Judges might undergo a process of 'case-hardening' where they are less likely to believe an accused because they have been exposed to so many cases.

[122] See Leverick 2020 for a summary of research on rape myths.

[123] For example, see Slater 2023.   [124] This list has been adapted from Ross 2023c.

- intra-jury bias, where interpersonal biases affect the quality of deliberation (for example, jurors sidelining or being dominated by certain participants).

(II)   Jurors fail to understand their legal role or the legal parameters constraining their decision. For example, they might not understand judicial directions, the standard of proof, or the distinction between the *actus reus* and *mens rea*.

(III) Jurors are susceptible to misunderstand the evidence presented in court, especially when it is complex (as in a fraud trial) or contains statistical components (as with DNA evidence).

(IV)   Jurors are susceptible to 'manipulation' – for example, by lawyerly rhetoric, gruesome evidence, and other aspects of trial strategy that do not reliably uncover the truth.

We might hope that we can rely on empirical evidence to know the extent to which juries exhibit these failings, perhaps hoping that psychologists and other researchers can tell us how well or badly jurors typically perform. However, although there is much written on the performance of the jury, there are good reasons to be cautious about relying on much extant evidence.

As we noted in our discussion of nullification (Section 5.4), jury deliberations are secret. In some jurisdictions, it is a criminal offence to reveal what happens in the jury room. Elsewhere, institutional barriers prevent researchers from working with real juries.[125] Apart from a few small exceptions, no jurisdiction has conducted substantial research into live deliberation of real jurors.[126]

This means that a striking fact about jury research is that, for the most part, it is not being carried out on real juries engaged in live deliberation about genuine trials. The most common alternative to this problem is to conduct research on what are called 'mock juries' instead.[127] Mock juries are members of the public who actively volunteer to take part in faux trials. The faux trials range in sophistication; the most common involve having participants read a written story and fill in a questionnaire, while the most realistic involve partial re-enactments of trials involving actors.[128] From these studies, researchers try to work out how juries might perform under real trial conditions.

---

[125] For example, see Horan and Israel 2016.   [126] But see Vidmar et al. 2003.

[127] Another type of research, which is less common, surveys real jurors about their experiences after the trial has finished. For an illustrative example, see Thomas 2020. See Chalmers, Leverick, and Munro 2021 for a methodological discussion of this approach.

[128] Mock jury studies can be realistic; for example, see Thomas 2010 or Ormston et al. 2019. But these are rare.

Should we worry about the fact that jury research does not involve real trials?[129] There are different views, with some arguing that mock juries and other indirect methods are suitably reliable indicators of real-life performance, while others remain sceptical that we can learn about the real thing through mere simulations. There are some advantages to the use of mock juries, the most important being that they allow for investigators to change variables in a targeted way. For example, you might try to work out whether there are gender differences in reactions to trials by exposing differently composed juries to the exact same material. You couldn't do this with a real jury – you just have to make do with the trials as they occur naturally. But there are also some serious objections to mock-jury research.[130]

The most important concern is about what psychologists call 'ecological validity': the extent to which we should expect behaviour under the artificial conditions of an experiment to generalise to real-world behaviour. I think there are reasons to be pessimistic about how much we can learn from mock-jury studies.[131] The big difference between mock-jury studies and real juries is that real juries are making decisions that have genuine – sometimes literally life-and-death – importance, while mock juries are just engaging in hypothetical discussion. Indeed, in a mock-jury study, there will typically not be a 'right' answer. Do people use different decision-making strategies when their decision has real-world importance? If the answer is 'yes', then we should not be confident that mock-jury studies reflect the behaviour of real-life juries.

The solution to this problem would be for governments to facilitate research into real juries deliberating live about genuine criminal trials. Such research could be relatively unobtrusive, such as transcribing deliberations, making it anonymous, and allowing researchers to have access after a few years. Some worry that even such modest steps would be too much interference with the jury and infringe the right of the accused to a fair trial. I find these arguments hard to understand. After all, the choice about whether to keep, reform, or abolish trial by jury is a long-term decision of deep social significance. Given the importance of criminal justice, it seems there is a moral imperative to make the decision about who should decide trials based on the best possible evidence.

---

[129] These worries are deepened by the fact that psychology has been facing a crisis concerning the reliability of empirical studies.

[130] I develop this argument in Ross 2023c. For a brief summary, see Ross 2023d.

[131] I have recently argued for a new type of research into jury deliberation where mock juries are exposed to real trials as they occur (rather than to faux trial reproductions). This would significantly improve on many current studies by making for a maximally realistic experimental subject experience. For details and comprehensive discussion of jury research, see Ross in press.

Of course, if it did turn out that juries were somewhat biased, misunderstood legal concepts, or exhibited other 'unreliable' tendencies, we would need to work out how to react. One way might be to offer better guidance or training to juries (if we thought that such training would work and be sufficiently value-neutral). But at some point we could be confronted with the questions with which we began this section, questions that are more philosophical. To what extent do the other strengths of the jury – for instance, as a safeguard against state oppression or as the 'conscience of the community' – compensate for other errors juries may be disposed to make? These are truly hard questions.

Overall, I am an optimist about trial by jury. But juries are rightly controversial and legal systems can function effectively without them. The values at stake are hard to weigh against each other. The reader should expect the debate on the use of juries to remain a central question in applied philosophy of law.

References

Abramson, Jeffrey. 1993. 'The Jury and Democratic Theory'. *Journal of Political Philosophy* 1, no. 1: 45–68.

Adams, N. P. 2023. 'Bare Statistical Evidence and the Right to Security'. *Journal of Ethics and Social Philosophy* 24, no. 2. https://doi.org/10.26556/jesp.v24i2.1650.

Angwin, Julia, Jeff Larson, Lauren Kirchner, and Surya Mattu. 2016. 'Machine Bias'. *ProPublica*. www.propublica.org/article/machine-bias-risk-assessments-in-criminal-sentencing, accessed 27 April 2023.

Baker, John. 2019. *Introduction to English Legal History*. Fifth edition .Oxford: Oxford University Press.

Beccaria, Cesare. 1995. 'Beccaria: "On Crimes and Punishments" and Other Writings'. Edited by Richard Bellamy. Translated by Richard Davies. Cambridge Texts in the History of Political Thought Cambridge: Cambridge University Press. https://bit.ly/3Or7mfa, accessed 5 February 2024.

Bindler, Anna, and Randi Hjalmarsson. 2018. 'How Punishment Severity Affects Jury Verdicts: Evidence from Two Natural Experiments'. *American Economic Journal: Economic Policy* 10, no. 4: 36–78.

Blackstone, William. 1827. *Commentaries on the Laws of England*. Philadelphia, PA: J. Grigg.

Blome-Tillmann, Michael. 2017. 'More Likely Than Not'. In Adam Carter, Emma Gordon, and Benjamin Jarvis, eds., *Knowledge First: Approaches in Epistemology and Mind*. Oxford: Oxford University Press, 278–92.

2020. 'Statistical Evidence, Normalcy, and the Gatecrasher Paradox'. *Mind* 129, no. 514: 563–78.

Bolinger, Renée Jorgensen. 2020. 'The Rational Impermissibility of Accepting (Some) Racial Generalizations'. *Synthese* 197, no. 6: 2415–31.

Bray, Samuel. 2005. 'Not Proven: Introducing a Third Verdict'. *University of Chicago Law Review* 72, no. 4: 1299–329.

Brennan, Jason, and Peter Martin Jaworski. 2015. 'Markets without Symbolic Limits'. *Ethics* 125, no. 4: 1053–77.

Brooks, Thom. 2004. 'A Defence of Jury Nullification'. *Res Publica* 10: 401–23.

Buchak, Lara. 2014. 'Belief, Credence, and Norms'. *Philosophical Studies* 169, no. 2: 285–311.

Burd, Kayla A., and Valerie P. Hans. 2018. 'Reasoned Verdicts: Oversold?' *Cornell International Law Journal* 51, no. 2: 319–60.

Butler, Sara M. 2019. 'More than Mothers: Juries of Matrons and Pleas of the Belly in Medieval England'. *Law and History Review* 37, no. 2: 353–96.

Chalfin, Aaron, and Justin McCrary. 2017. 'Criminal Deterrence: A Review of the Literature'. *Journal of Economic Literature* 55, no. 1: 5–48.

Chalmers, James, Fiona Leverick, and Vanessa Munro. 2021. 'Why the Jury Is, and Should Still Be, out on Rape Deliberation'. *Criminal Law Review* 9: 753–71.

2022. 'Beyond Doubt: The Case against "Not Proven"'. *Modern Law Review* 85, no. 4: 847–78.

Coen, Mark, and Jonathan Doak. 2017. 'Embedding Explained Jury Verdicts in the English Criminal Trial'. *Legal Studies* 37, no. 4: 786–806.

Cohen, Laurence Jonathan. 1977. *The Probable and the Provable*. Oxford: Oxford University Press.

Conee, Earl, and Richard Feldman. 1998. 'The Generality Problem for Reliabilism'. *Philosophical Studies* 89, no. 1: 1–29.

Di Bello, Marcello. 2020. 'Proof Paradoxes and Normic Support: Socializing or Relativizing?' *Mind* 129, no. 516: 1269–85.

Ebert, Philip A., Martin Smith, and Ian Durbach. 2018. 'Lottery Judgments: A Philosophical and Experimental Study'. *Philosophical Psychology* 31, no. 1: 110–38.

Enoch, David, and Levi Spectre. 2019. 'Sensitivity, Safety, and the Law: A Reply to Pardo'. Hebrew University of Jerusalem Legal Research Paper 20–28. http://dx.doi.org/10.2139/ssrn.3462424.

Enoch, David, Talia Fisher, and Levi Spectre. 2021. 'Does Legal Epistemology Rest on a Mistake? On Fetishism, Two-Tier System Design, and Conscientious Fact-finding'. *Philosophical Issues* 31, no. 1: 85–103.

Enoch, David, Levi Spectre, and Talia Fisher. 2012. 'Statistical Evidence, Sensitivity, and the Legal Value of Knowledge'. *Philosophy & Public Affairs* 40, no. 3: 197–224.

Epps, Daniel. 2015. 'The consequences of Error in Criminal Justice'. *Harvard Law Review* 128, no. 4: 1065–1151.

Fisher, Talia. 2021. 'Half the Guilt'. *Theoretical Inquiries in Law* 22, no. 1: 87–109.

Full Fact. 2019. 'How Many Rapists Reoffend?' Website. https://fullfact.org/crime/how-many-rapists-reoffend/, acceesed 6 March 2024.

Gardiner, Georgi. 2017. 'In Defence of Reasonable Doubt'. *Journal of Applied Philosophy* 34, no. 2: 221–41.

2019. 'The Reasonable and the Relevant: Legal Standards of Proof'. *Philosophy & Public Affairs* 47, no. 3: 288–318.

Gardner, J. 2015. 'The Many Faces of the Reasonable Person'. *Law Quarterly Review* 131, October: 563–84.

Gendler, Tamar Szabó. 2011. 'On the Epistemic Costs of Implicit Bias'. *Philosophical Studies: An International Journal for Philosophy in the Analytic Tradition* 156, no. 1: 33–63.

Hedden, Brian R. 2017. 'Should Juries Deliberate?' *Social Epistemology* 31, no. 4: 368–86.

Hedden, Brian, and Mark Colyvan. 2019. 'Legal Probabilism: A Qualified Defence'. *Journal of Political Philosophy* 27, no. 4: 448–68.

HM Government. 2021. *The End-to-End Rape Review Report on Findings and Actions*. https://bit.ly/4a16ara.

Horan, Jacqueline, and Mark Israel. 2016. 'Beyond the Legal Barriers: Institutional Gatekeeping and Real Jury Research'. *Australian & New Zealand Journal of Criminology* 49, no. 3: 422–36.

Huemer, Michael. 2018. 'The Duty to Disregard the Law'. *Criminal Law and Philosophy* 12, no. 1: 1–18.

Kaplan, John. 1968. 'Decision Theory and the Factfinding Process'. *Stanford Law Review* 20, no. 6: 1065–92.

Kim, Brian. 2017. 'Pragmatic Encroachment in Epistemology'. *Philosophy Compass* 12, no. 5: e12415. https://doi.org/10.1111/phc3.12415.

Kitai, Rinat. 2003. 'Protecting the Guilty'. *Buffalo Criminal Law Review* 6, no. 2: 1163–87.

Krauss, Sam Fox. 2020. 'Against the Alleged Insufficiency of Statistical Evidence'. *Florida State University Law Review* 47: 801–25.

Lackey, Jennifer. 2021. 'Norms of Criminal Conviction'. *Philosophical Issues* 31, no. 1: 188–209.

Landemore, Hélène. 2013. 'Deliberation, Cognitive Diversity, and Democratic Inclusiveness: An Epistemic Argument for the Random Selection of Representatives'. *Synthese* 190, no. 7: 1209–31.

Laudan, Larry. 2003. 'Is Reasonable Doubt Reasonable?' *Legal Theory* 9, no. 4: 295–331. https://doi.org/10.1017/S1352325203000132.

2006. *Truth, Error, and Criminal Law: An Essay in Legal Epistemology.* Cambridge: Cambridge University Press.

2011. 'The Rules of Trial, Political Morality, and the Costs of Error: Or, Is Proof Beyond a Reasonable Doubt Doing More Harm than Good?' In Leslie Green and Brian Leiter, eds., *Oxford Studies in Philosophy of Law.* New York: Oxford University Press, 195–227.

Lee, Youngjae. 2018. 'The Criminal Jury, Moral Judgments, and Political Representation'. *University of Illinois Law Review,* 1255–91.

Levanon, Liat. 2022. *Evidence, Respect and Truth.* Oxford: Bloomsbury Publishing. www.bloomsbury.com/uk/evidence-respect-and-truth-9781509942657/, accessed 27 April 2023.

Leverick, Fiona. 2020. 'What Do We Know about Rape Myths and Juror Decision Making?' *International Journal of Evidence & Proof* 24, no. 3: 255–79.

Lillquist, Erik. 2002. 'Recasting Reasonable Doubt: Decision Theory and the Virtues of Variability'. *UC Davis Law Review* 36, no. 1: 85–198.

Lippke, Richard. 2010. 'Punishing the Guilty, Not Punishing the Innocent'. *Journal of Moral Philosophy* 7, no. 4: 462–88.

Littlejohn, Clayton. 2020. 'Truth, Knowledge, and the Standard of Proof in Criminal Law'. *Synthese* 197, no. 12: 5253–86.

Loeb, Don, and Sebastián Reyes Molina. 2022. 'Standards of Proof as Competence Norms'. *Jurisprudence* 13, no. 3: 349–69.

Loftus, Elizabeth F. 1996. *Eyewitness Testimony: With a New Preface*. Cambridge, MA: Harvard University Press.

McConnell, D. 2021. 'A Jurors Guide to Going Rogue'. *Practical Ethics*, 14 May. http://blog.practicalethics.ox.ac.uk/2021/05/a-jurors-guide-to-going-rogue/, accessed 6 March 2024.

McDonald, J. H. A. 1948. *Practical Treatise on the Criminal Law of Scotland*. Fifth edition. Edinburgh: W. Green.

Melchior, Guido. 2019. *Knowing and Checking: An Epistemological Investigation*. New York: Routledge.

Mill, John Stuart. 2010. *Considerations on Representative Government*. Cambridge: Cambridge University Press. https://doi.org/10.1017/CBO9780511783128.

Mortini, Dario. 2022. 'Knowledge, Individualised Evidence and Luck'. *Philosophical Studies* 179, no. 12: 3791–3815.

Moss, Sarah. 2022. 'Knowledge and Legal Proof'. In Tamar Szabó Gendler, John Hawthorne, and Julianne Chung, eds., *Oxford Studies in Epistemology: Volume 7*. Oxford: Oxford University Press, 176–213. https://doi.org/10.1093/oso/9780192868978.003.0006.

Nagin, Daniel S. 2013. 'Deterrence in the Twenty-First Century'. *Crime and Justice* 42, no. 1: 199–263.

Neumann, Nico, Ulf Böckenholt, and Ashish Sinha. 2016. 'A Meta-Analysis of Extremeness Aversion'. *Journal of Consumer Psychology* 26, no. 2: 193–212.

Nunn, G. 2015. 'The Incompatibility of Due Process and Naked Statistical Evidence'. *Vanderbilt Law Review* 68, no. 5: 1407–33.

Ormston, Rachel, James Chalmers, Fiona Leverick, Vanessa Munro, and Lorraine Murray. 2019. *Scottish Jury Research: Findings from a Large Scale Mock Jury Study*. Edinburgh: Scottish Government. https://bit.ly/3whszSo, accessed February 14, 2024.

Pardo, Michael S. 2018. 'Safety vs. Sensitivity: Possible Worlds and the Law of Evidence'. *Legal Theory* 24, no. 1: 50–75.

Paternoster, Raymond. 2010. 'How Much Do We Really Know about Criminal Deterrence?' *Criminal Law & Criminology* 100, no. 3: 765–823.

Picinali, Federico. 2022. *Justice In-Between: A Study of Intermediate Criminal Verdicts*. Oxford: Oxford University Press.

Pritchard, Duncan. 2009. 'Safety-Based Epistemology: Wither Now?' *Journal of Philosophical Research* 34: 33–45.

2022. 'In Defence of the Modal Account of Legal Risk'. *Synthese* 200, no. 290. https://doi.org/10.1007/s11229-022-03693-z

Pundik, Amit. 2008. 'Statistical Evidence and Individual Litigants: A Reconsideration of Wasserman's Argument from Autonomy'. *International Journal of Evidence & Proof* 12, no. 4: 303–24.

2022. 'Should Murder Be More Difficult to Prove than Theft? Beccaria and Differential Standards of Proof'. In Antje du Bois-Pedain and Shachar Eldar, eds., *Re-Reading Beccaria: On the Contemporary Significance of a Penal Classic*. Oxford: Hart Publishing, 199–214. https://bit.ly/49zaCNp, accessed 14 February 2024.

Rabin, Yoram, and Yaniv Vaki. 2023. 'Acquittal on the Basis of Doubt – A Call for its Abolition'. *Haifa Law Review* 17, no. 1. https://bit.ly/3P9SP81, accessed 6 March 2024.

Rape Crisis Scotland. (n.d.). 'End Not Proven'. Website. www.rapecrisisscotland.org.uk/campaigns-end-not-proven/.

Redmayne, Mike. 2008. 'Exploring the Proof Paradoxes'. *Legal Theory* 14, no. 4: 281–309.

Ribeiro, Gustavo. 2019. 'The Case for Varying Standards of Proof'. *San Diego Law Review* 56, no. 1: 161–219.

Ross, Lewis. 2020. 'Recent Work on the Proof Paradox'. *Philosophy Compass* 15, no. 6: e12667. https://doi.org/10.1111/phc3.12667.

2021a. 'Rehabilitating Statistical Evidence'. *Philosophy and Phenomenological Research* 102, no. 1: 3–23.

2021b. 'Legal Proof and Statistical Conjunctions'. *Philosophical Studies* 178, no. 6: 2021–41.

2021c. 'Justice in Epistemic Gaps: The "Proof Paradox" Revisited'. *Philosophical Issues* 31, no. 1: 315–33.

2022. Profiling, Neutrality, and Social Equality'. *Australasian Journal of Philosophy* 100, no. 4: 808–24.

2023a. 'The Foundations of Criminal Law Epistemology'. *Ergo* 9, no. 58: 1581–1603. https://doi.org/10.3998/ergo.3583.

2023b. 'Criminal Proof: Fixed or Flexible?' *Philosophical Quarterly* 73, no. 4: 1077–99. https://doi.org/10.1093/pq/pqad001.

2023c. 'The Curious Case of the Jury-Shaped Hole: A Plea for Real Jury Research'. *International Journal of Evidence & Proof* 27, no. 2: 107–25. https://doi.org/10.1177/13657127221150451.

2023d. 'Jury Reform and Live Deliberation Research'. *Amicus Curiae* 5, no. 1: 64–70. https://journals.sas.ac.uk/amicus/article/view/5661/5325.

In press. 'Mock Juries, Real Trials: How to Solve (Some) Problems with Jury Science'. *Journal of Law and Society*.

Roth, Andrea. 2010. 'Safety in Numbers – Deciding When DNA Alone Is Enough to Convict'. *New York University Law Review* 85: 1130–85.

Sand, Leonard B., and Danielle L. Rose. 2003. 'Proof beyond All Possible Doubt: Is There a Need for Higher Burden of Proof When the Sentence May Be Death?' *Chicago-Kent Law Review* 78, no. 3: 1359–78.

Shapiro, Barbara J. 1986. 'To a Moral Certainty: Theories of Knowledge and Anglo-American Juries 1600–1850'. *Hastings Law Journal* 38, no. 1: 153–93.

Siscoe, Robert W. 2022. 'Condorcet's Jury Theorem and Democracy'. *1000-Word Philosophy*, 20 July. https://1000wordphilosophy.com/2022/07/20/condorcets-jury-theorem/.

Slater, Joe. 2023. 'Just Judge: The Jury on Trial'. *American Philosophical Quarterly* 60, no. 2: 169–86.

Smith, Martin. 2016. *Between Probability and Certainty: What Justifies Belief.* Oxford: Oxford Academic. https://doi.org/10.1093/acprof:oso/9780198755333.001.0001.

2018. 'When Does Evidence Suffice for Conviction?' *Mind* 127, no. 508: 1193–1218.

2020. 'Against Legal Probabilism'. In Jon Robson and Zachary Hoskins, eds., *The Social Epistemology of Legal Trials.* Abingdon, UK: Routledge, 92–105.

Solan, Lawrence. 1999. 'Refocusing the Burden of Proof in Criminal Cases: Some Doubt About Reasonable Doubt'. *Texas Law Review* 78: 105–47.

Sosa, Ernest. 1999. 'How to Defeat Opposition to Moore'. *Philosophical Perspectives* 13: 141–53.

Spottswood, Mark. 2021. 'Continuous Burdens of Proof'. *Nevada Law Journal* 21, no. 2. https://scholars.law.unlv.edu/nlj/vol21/iss2/9, accessed 14 February 2024.

Sunstein, Cass R. 2021. 'Governing by Algorithm? No Noise and (Potentially) Less Bias'. Harvard Public Law Working Paper no. 21–35. http://dx.doi.org/10.2139/ssrn.3925240.

Thomas, Cheryl. 2010. 'Are Juries Fair?' Ministry of Justice Research Series 1/10. https://bit.ly/437pCA1.

2020. 'The 21st Century Jury: Contempt, Bias and the Impact of Jury Service'. *Criminal Law Review* 11: 987–1011.

2023. 'Juries, Rape and Sexual Offences in the Crown Court 2007–21'. *Criminal Law Review* 3: 200–25.

Tribe, Laurence H. 1971. 'Trial by Mathematics: Precision and Ritual in the Legal Process'. *Harvard Law Review* 84, no. 6: 1329. https://api.seman ticscholar.org/CorpusID:14731357, accessed 14 February 2024.

Urbaniak, Rafal, and Marcello Di Bello. 2021. 'Legal Probabilism'. In Edward N. Zalta, ed., *The Stanford Encyclopedia of Philosophy*. https:// plato.stanford.edu/archives/fall2021/entries/legal-probabilism/, accessed 27 April 2023.

Vaki, Yaniv, and Yoram Rabin. 2021. 'Two Kinds of Acquittals – Different Kinds of Doubts'. *Criminal Law Forum* 32, no. 1: 97–123.

Vidmar, Neil, Shari Diamond, Mary Rose, and René Ellis. 2003. 'Juror Discussions during Civil Trials: Studying an Arizona Innovation'. *Arizona Law Review* 45: 1–83.

Volokh, Alexander. 1997. 'N Guilty Men'. University of Pennsylvania Law Review 146, no.2. https://papers.ssrn.com/abstract=11412, accessed 15 February 2023.

Walen, Alec D. 2015. 'Proof beyond a Reasonable Doubt: A Balanced Retributive Account'. *Louisiana Law Review* 76: 355–456.

Wasserman, David T. 1992. 'The Morality of Statistical Proof and the Risk of Mistaken Liability Decision and Interference Litigation'. *Cardozo Law Review* 13, no. 2–3: 935–76.

Wells, Gary L. 1992. 'Naked Statistical Evidence of Liability: Is Subjective Probability Enough?' *Journal of Personality and Social Psychology* 62, no. 5: 739–52.

Williamson, Timothy. 2000. *Knowledge and Its Limits*. Oxford: Oxford University Press.

Woollard, Fiona, and Frances Howard-Snyder. 2022. 'Doing vs. Allowing Harm'. In Edward N. Zalta and Uri Nodelman, eds., *The Stanford Encyclopedia of Philosophy*. https://plato.stanford.edu/archives/win2022/ entries/doing-allowing/, accessed 27 April 2023.

Worsnip, Alex. 2021. 'Can Pragmatists Be Moderate?' *Philosophy and Phenomenological Research* 102, no. 3: 531–58.

Cambridge Elements $\equiv$

Philosophy of Law

Series Editors

George Pavlakos
University of Glasgow

George Pavlakos is Professor of Law and Philosophy at the School of Law, University of Glasgow. He has held visiting posts at the universities of Kiel and Luzern, the European University Institute, the UCLA Law School, the Cornell Law School and the Beihang Law School in Beijing. He is the author of *Our Knowledge of the Law* (2007) and more recently has co-edited *Agency, Negligence and Responsibility* (2021) and *Reasons and Intentions in Law and Practical Agency* (2015).

Gerald J. Postema
University of North Carolina at Chapel Hill

Gerald J. Postema is Professor Emeritus of Philosophy at the University of North Carolina at Chapel Hill. Among his publications count *Utility, Publicity, and Law: Bentham's Moral and Legal Philosophy* (2019); *On the Law of Nature, Reason, and the Common Law: Selected Jurisprudential Writings of Sir Matthew Hale* (2017); *Legal Philosophy in the Twentieth Century: The Common Law World* (2011), *Bentham and the Common Law Tradition*, 2nd edition (2019).

Kenneth M. Ehrenberg
University of Surrey

Kenneth M. Ehrenberg is Professor of Jurisprudence and Philosophy at the University of Surrey School of Law and Co-Director of the Surrey Centre for Law and Philosophy. He is the author of *The Functions of Law* (2016) and numerous articles on the nature of law, jurisprudential methodology, the relation of law to morality, practical authority, and the epistemology of evidence law.

Associate Editor

Sally Zhu
University of Sheffield

Sally Zhu is a Lecturer in Property Law at University of Sheffield. Her research is on property and private law aspects of platform and digital economies.

About the Series

This series provides an accessible overview of the philosophy of law, drawing on its varied intellectual traditions in order to showcase the interdisciplinary dimensions of jurisprudential enquiry, review the state of the art in the field, and suggest fresh research agendas for the future. Focussing on issues rather than traditions or authors, each contribution seeks to deepen our understanding of the foundations of the law, ultimately with a view to offering practical insights into some of the major challenges of our age.

Cambridge Elements ☰

Philosophy of Law

Elements in the Series

A full series listing is available at: www.cambridge.org/EPHL

Printed in the United States
by Baker & Taylor Publisher Services